RUNNING WATERS

Books by Datus Proper

What the Trout Said

Pheasants of the Mind

The Last Old Place

Running Waters

RUNNING WATERS

Datus Proper

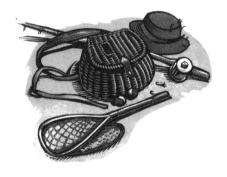

The Lyons Press
Guilford, Connecticut
An Imprint of The Globe Pequot Press

The Lyons Press is an imprint of The Globe Pequot Press.

Printed in United States of America
Designed by A Good Thing Inc.

10 9 8 7 6 5 4 3 2 1

Library of Congress Cataloguing-in-Publication Data is available on file.

For Nick Lyons—

godfather of this brainchild

CONTENTS

Up the Mountain
and into the Stream

Some people think of trout as food. Mention trout to a Russian, for example, and you may be told to roll your fish in flour and cook them, heads and all, in sputtering butter. But that is the last recipe on these pages.

Most anglers, in our American state of abundance, can afford to forget about a fish dinner—at least until the sun sets and a cold mist puts an end to the evening rise. While there is still light, we want to know what fly the trout are eating, so that we can tie on an imitation with a hook in it. We are caught up in one of life's miracles—beautiful fish sipping beautiful insects.

And here is the conundrum. We love trout, mayflies, and cool streams not because they fit on our degraded planet but because they are remnants of something better. We love that something, and so we fight for it. Without anglers, there would be even more pollution and more dams, both of which make sense in a backward world. Trout are a drag on profits.

The rest of this gets awkward—like telling my wife why I come home early, sometimes, while trout are still rising. The attraction is not her carrot cake, though it is the world's best. I am not even attracted to her dress, though it is speckled like a brook trout. No. What brings me home is something primitive, indescribable, and irresistible.

Fishing is the same. There must be a hunter-gatherer's hormone buried deep under the debris of civilization—some ancient drive that pulls anglers up the mountains and into the streams.

Yesterday, though, I pushed my luck. Light was fading on the tallest peaks and the canyon was dark when I packed my waders in a rucksack, groped around for my rod, and could not find it. I felt almost as if I had let my wife down. That rod was part of me too—a gentle old friend of first-generation graphite with four-ounce reel, lost in a tangle of willows while I changed my boots for the hike out.

And then this morning I was back in the mountains at first light and the rod was there, in plain view. Any hiker could have spotted it and taken it home. But no one else would have had its story.

Running Waters has stories about people who have become friends because of rivers; rivers themselves that have become friends; the ways of trout and flies; the fish themselves and the discrete ways of the several species. *Running Waters* does not offer final answers to the multitude of trout-fishing problems—but I hope it offers a balanced view of matters that have concerned me since I wrote *What the Trout Said*, nearly twenty years ago.

DATUS PROPER
Gallatin Valley, Montana
January 2001

PART ONE

People of the Stream

Dark Hollow

Fish a place long enough and it becomes a homestead, a personal stretch of boulders and water and trout. I've been proving my claim on Dark Hollow Run for twenty years now. You will understand, therefore, that I wondered about the other car parked on Skyline Drive, right where I always start my hike down to the stream. Maybe the visitor was just the usual refugee from the cities, out for a stroll on the Appalachian Trail, but then again I might find a fisherman ahead of me. I hurried down the mountainside with my rod and rucksack.

The other visitor was easy to catch. "Hill's getting hard to pull," she said. Her hair was more gray than red where it fell over the lace collar of her dress. Her name was Betty Cave, and her only burden was a bunch of flowers, but it established a claim 200 years older than mine. I read the names of her family when we got to what used to be the Dark Hollow settlement. There were more headstones in the clearing than Betty had flowers to decorate—rough fieldstones, big ones for the adults and little ones, lots of little ones. One of the unmarked stones was for the Cave who brought the family's red hair from Ireland to the Blue Ridge long ago. The oldest legible marker was for John G. Cave of the Virginia Light Artillery, C.S.A. Near it there were stones for Betty's parents and her sister Lula Belle.

Not far away was a fireplace, stones chinked with mud, standing lonely in the woods. Betty Cave had stories to go with that old hearth. It had been part of her family's cabin, once, and she remembered the days when her mother tended the fire and her father came home with food.

Daddy used to bring a leather pouch with trout spilling over the top. He caught 'em on worms—big fish, like this—a foot long, some of 'em. They was real pretty. Mama cleaned 'em all and kept 'em cool in a stone jar in the spring house. The meat was pink when she cooked 'em. They tasted awful good.

I strung up my rod, tied on a little dark-water fly, and worked upstream making back casts, when I could, but otherwise just pushing the line out. This sounds impossible—like pushing a string—but you get good at push-casting on Dark Hollow Run. When there is brush behind, you just pile line on the water at your feet, hold the rod straight up, and make half a roll cast, the forward half. It's not a way to break distance records. The line goes where the rod tip points, though, and the fish are not far away. The little fly rights itself, shimmies its peacock body at the trout, and flashes you a V-for-victory sign with white wings. You hold the rod tip high so that the line does not get caught in the fast water at the tail of the pool. You want the fly to take life easy, like a big trout.

Watching a good fly is like watching a bird dog that knows what it's doing. You have faith. Almost every pool has at least a small fish—in the middle, where a trout can hold in slow water and foray into the current for a passing snack, or in the calm patch above a boulder, or in little eddies at the head of the pool. When the fly dallies over just the right spot, the fish responds. A little one is a sparkle, making up its mind and pouncing in the same instant. A big trout is a shadow, a lovely lazy rise without fuss.

The old-timers all say that the fish used to run larger than they do now. Betty Cave tends to understatement, like most of the mountain people, and you must not dismiss her foot-long trout as yarn spinning. I don't know what has changed the ecology of the stream. Acid rain is probably involved and so are the young oaks and maples, which drink up moisture that used to reach the Run. There was more water for the fish when the Caves lived in Dark Hollow.

We had 400 acres, all grass but for the orchard and the hemlocks around the house. We kept the brush cut down till the government made us leave. We grazed six heifers and a horse and two milk cows, and Mama stored the butter in the spring house.

Grandma planted that snowball bush, too. It blooms every June, and the apple trees still set fruit, but the pears and peaches are shaded out now. Mama used to can all the fruit. Mama and Daddy worked hard but we weren't hungry.

I worked hard too, sneaking up to the tails of pools, sitting on a rock to keep my head below the trout's line of sight, and planning before I cast. The brook trout that took the fly were two-year-olds about 7 inches long. I rose none of the big three-year-olds. The concentration was tiring, more so than the walk down the mountain. I was relieved to reach the Lunch Pool, sit on a patch of moss, and pull out my food.

The Lunch Pool is one of those places that just grew around me over the years. Maybe it was in the middle of my homestead water because I deserved a break, or maybe I staked my claim knowing that the pool was available. The sycamore tree beat me there by a long time, anyhow. It may have been growing even in the days of Great-Grandfather Cave. The trunk was as thick as four Dark Hollow girls standing back to back, pale toes wriggling down into the pool.

I ate each of my rye crackers with a sardine dripping oil on it, and halfway through lunch there was a grumble over the ridge to the south. Dark clouds moved overhead fast, but the thunder stayed lazy. A few raindrops made rings in the pool while I rushed through my apple, and then there was another ring made from below the water rather than above. I stripped line off the reel and covered the fish with one false cast, not standing up. The trout drifted under the fly and took it and pulled with a strength almost unseemly on such a small battlefield. Then the fish gave up and lay in my left hand. Both its mouth and its girth were big for its length of 9½ inches, and its belly was the deep red-orange of a maple tree. This was a three-year-old, survivor of two spawning seasons but programmed by its genes to die before another. It died instead for my wife's dinner.

The shower was steady, by then, and I wasted no time.

Another good fish took my fly in the next pool, but the hook lost its grip. I changed to a fly with more clearance between point of hook and fat herl body, and in the two pools upstream I caught two more big fish, which meant that my wife and I could both have dinner. That's how it goes on Dark Hollow Run: You can fish for hours without a venerable trout, but the first shower gives you satisfaction.

The old fish hide when the water gets low. Then the rain comes and they move out, chase the small fry away from the best spots in the pools, and lie in wait, tails moving, eyes looking up. Even the first few raindrops revive some genetic recollection of the wetter, colder climate Betty Cave describes.

I let the cat out one time and it froze in the snow before it got back in. I cried and cried.

My daddy hiked down to the old copper mine for work in winter. He didn't have no boots—had to put socks over his shoes and tie them up with tar strings. The snow was so deep that his clothes was froze up to his waist when he got home. We were happy to get the money.

There was eight cabins in Dark Hollow, then, and the church. They was awful good people, good Christian people. Daddy went around with a lantern in the snow when the diphtheria came. He visited the houses of sick people to pray. Two children died the same day. Daddy had to cut up a church bench to make a coffin for them.

The climb back up through the woods to Skyline Drive was slow, my excuse being that I wanted to take an inventory of my homestead. Rain made that easier, too. The violets stood straighter, the wild geraniums glowed pink-purple, and the first white trilliums began to open. In what was left of the orchard at Betty Cave's old place, a mountain pheasant twisted off through gray trunks. We call them ruffed grouse now. I saw no woodcock, but farther along the path a gray squirrel darted to the back side of its tree and I wondered why it was so spooky till a goshawk buzzed me. Its nest must have been nearby, with young hungry for small game.

Two bunches of deer, on the other hand, stood watching me tamely. Deer have become too abundant for their forage, recently—a problem common in the national parks. Hunting is not allowed and there are not enough big predators to control populations.

I don't remember deer in the 'thirties. Never heard Daddy name a deer, but he hunted mountain pheasants here in the hollow and walked to Big Meadow to shoot wood hens. They was funny little birds with long bills and round heads and big eyes.

We heard a mountain panther screamin' and hollerin' like a baby, one time, and our dog was so scared we let him inside. I looked out the window and saw the panther coming closeter and closeter. It had eyes like a piece of fire.

A bear broke down our smokehouse one night and stole a ham. Daddy tracked the bear down but he told me he didn't kill it, because I didn't like anything to get hurt. We had plenty of ham left, I remember. Wonder if some of it came from that bear.

Daddy tracked rabbits and squirrels with his little dog, and they did smell good when Mama cooked 'em. I remember she baked raccoons, too, with potatoes and carrots from the garden. We ate the mushrats and sold their hides. We didn't eat 'possums, but some folks did—fattened them up and cooked 'em.

Change would have come to the old settlement, in time, even if the old families had been allowed to stay in their homes. Somebody would have driven a car to the cabins and the world would have followed, one vehicle at a time. People who had been part of nature would have erected television antennas in the heart of Dark Hollow.

With humans gone, the original vegetation returned, and if the young hardwoods drank some of the stream's water, they also protected the watershed from erosion. The trout were not big, but they were doing better here than in most parts of their ancestral range. I expected to find the native wildlife waiting for me as long as I could manage the hard pull.

Something beautiful had been saved for me—and taken from the Caves.

When they first built Skyline Drive, I would hike up there and sell little paper flowers. Mama made 'em for me. I'd charge a dime, but some of the guests would stop their cars and give me a dollar. I was five years old.

After a while, the government pushed us off our land and made it part of Shenandoah National Park. That was before the war started—1939 or the edge of 1940, I think. Daddy got a dollar an acre. Friends gave us use of a house outside the park—they knew we couldn't pay rent. We wanted to go back to Dark Hollow but the government burnt down all eight cabins. Burnt the church, too.

Daddy didn't have any work. All he knew was farming and hunting and fishing. I remember him sitting outside every evening, cryin' and cryin'.

Bailey's Secret

Bailey Spigler took me fishing shortly after I first moved to Washington, D.C., and wanted to get away from it. On the first free Saturday I bought a license and followed the Potomac River upstream, but I didn't meet Bailey that day. Another old man was at the landing to rent boats and provide advice, which was a responsibility he took seriously. He told he that I would catch more smallmouth bass by wading if I did not mind getting wet.

I didn't. Fishing wasn't much with the water at 84° F, but I put a few little bass back and kept enough yellow-belly sunfish for dinner. The old man said that they would be better eating than bass. We talked awhile, and when he decided that I was all right, he told me that the best trout fisherman thereabouts was Bailey Spigler in Sharpsburg.

Bailey agreed to find me some trout. He may have recognized a sincerely desperate young fisherman when he heard one on the telephone. And then, too, Bailey may have reached the point in life when he welcomed recognition of his learning.

Next Saturday just after dawn I was at the door of Bailey's white frame house. I did not step inside or meet his family—never did, on that occasion or the others when I fished with him. People near the Mason-Dixon line liked privacy, in those days. There was nothing suburban about Sharpsburg yet, no barbecue grills or gift shops. There were small old houses, and Bailey just appeared at the door of one of them, hip boots on his feet, three-piece fly rod strung with line but broken down, bait hook up against the tip-top.

I drove while Bailey gave directions to a tiny tributary of Antietam Creek that did not look like trout water, and wasn't. There he unfurled a seine between two sticks, stuck their bottom ends in the gravel, and told me to herd some minnows downstream toward him. Two were in the net when he lifted it. Some folks settled for bait-shop shiners, Bailey said, but there was nothing like real stream-dwelling bull minnows to fool the trout. I suspected that he did not believe in wasting seventy-five cents on boughten bait, either.

We got to know each other during the half hour it took us to catch our minnows. Bailey was of average height and weight and his dark hair made him seem no more than middle-aged, but he did not move fast. What caught me was his good humor. I had thought of chasing minnows as just something that had to be done before we could go fishing, but Bailey took pleasure in the details: miniature pools and runs, a seine bagging in the current, warty little fish flapping in the meshes with mouths open but silent. We wound up admiring the trophies among bull minnows.

I had been afraid that everyone else would beat us to the big fish, but it was still early enough for mist to be rising from the Potomac River when we drove across it. Bailey mentioned that he knew of a few cool springs, deep in the bed of the river, and that in years gone by he had caught real brook trout there. He supposed that the native fish had drifted down from shady headwaters and taken refuge in the springs when the Potomac turned warm on its way to Washington. He thought that maybe he was the only man alive who still knew about those springs.

I wanted to look for the cold water right away, though I could not have said at the time why refugee trout seemed so desirable. I did have enough sense to back off when Bailey shook his head. Hadn't seen any of those big brook trout lately, he said. Maybe the pollution got them all.

He knew of a good place elsewhere, though. We bounced along a gravel road, paused on an iron bridge over Opequon Creek, and looked downstream. A fish boiled below a rapid—maybe just a fallfish (another warty creation) cornering bull minnows in the rapids. But I knew nothing of warm streams, and Bailey went along with my salmonid fantasies.

Then he parked and put together the pieces of his white steel fly rod, an antique even then. I was trying to get a 2-pound-test line through the guides of a light spinning rod. He gave me a hook like his and split our stock of bait, pouring my minnows into a marmalade jar. He took care to show me how the bait ought to be rigged, and I can picture the process still, hook going in the mouth and out through the gills and then back through again to form a loop. Then he pushed the hook through the minnow ahead of its tail and adjusted the loop until the body was pulled into a gentle curve by the leader. Bailey got tiny silver scales on his thumb and finger, and the minnow had a faint smell of stream-bottom mud.

Bailey waded into Opequon Creek then, me right behind him, and eased downstream to a place where the water ran deep and shady under the right bank. He stripped off thirty feet of a dark, level fly line and started roll casting the minnow toward the good spot. The old steel rod was heavy and slow, by modern standards—but it did not tear the bait. The line just cartwheeled out, and the minnow plopped down where he wanted it. Bailey let it sink a couple of feet, drifting downstream, and then retrieved it barely fast enough to make it turn over. I watched it flicker, sink, struggle ahead, flicker, sink. After about ten casts and ten yards of stream, Bailey dropped his rod tip. The floating line was pulled deeper into the water by a fish I had not seen. Bailey eased the line back through his fingers till he felt a heavy beat and then struck. The rod bent alarmingly, because there was not much spine to it, but that trout was as good as fried in cornmeal. It rolled and dived a couple of times and then lay in Bailey's net, wondering what had gone wrong with the world.

We admired the fish, and I remember that scene too. It's odd how some fragments of these old movies play back after more important memories have disappeared. Bailey's net had a rubber handle and a spring-steel bow that could be unscrewed and collapsed for travel. The meshes were of faded cotton. The fish was a rainbow, plump and good sized, almost a pound, but it was clearly a hatchery specimen, fins rounded, brain vestigial. It didn't hurt that Bailey knew exactly where the truck was wont to dump its load.

I moved off to do my own fishing then. My short rod was not as effective as Bailey's, but my line was good, a wispy monofilament that let me cast a bull minnow thirty feet with one split shot. The trout I remember was on the hook when Bailey stopped by to see how I was doing, and I was doing fine. A boy on the bank was telling me to haul the fish in before it wiggled loose, while Bailey explained that I couldn't horse a trout on 2-pound line. The boy was too excited to listen, what with all the splashing. Those man-made rainbows did not have much for brains, but they remembered how to pull.

Bailey and I fished together two or three more times that season and were contented in each other's company, mutually relieved to be with someone who understood the good things in life without explanation. Hatchery trout that I would have scorned in Montana seemed valuable when they pulled me away from a miasmal city. My memory may not be reliable in every respect, of course. Sometimes Bailey Spigler gets confused with all the other old men who saw something in me worth rescuing, but I think I have the important details right.

On our last trip of the season, Bailey guided me to a farm-house in an unpromising part of the West Virginia limestone country, right off U.S. 11, and there he talked to a man he'd evidently known for years. The farmer gave fishing permission and Bailey took it, which sounds one-sided, but the two seemed equally happy to see each other. This was before Americans had decided that spring-creek fishing was worth paying for.

Bailey went downstream and I up. The stream had been abused, like most others in the region—banks beaten down and bottom silted—but for all that, there was water buttercup waving in the current, and two trout spooked when I waded close. I sneaked up on the third before it saw me, and it was a real native. The event seemed miraculous, an apparition—little trout at the surface taking invisible insects, white-edged fins clear. I cast a $\frac{1}{16}$-ounce spinner far above the trout, brought it back glittering, and was almost relieved when the fish fled. Modern trinkets were all right for modern man-made trout but not for the real thing.

Bailey had two brook trout between 8 and 9 inches long—lovely fish, we agreed, if not as big as the ones that hid out in the Potomac springs. He had caught the pair on worms drifted underneath some brush. They lay in his creel, glistening on a comforter of ferns, and I admired them fervently. Bailey was as near ebullience as I'd ever seen him. Last year, he said, he'd been in the veteran's hospital at this season, and the doctors had not been sure that he would fish again. They'd treated him right, though. He had always been proud of fighting for his country in World War II, and he felt prouder than ever when he walked out of that hospital. He'd have been glad if I'd also caught a trout, but I was content to see the sun shining on Bailey alone. Nice day it was, too, wind from the west blowing off the haze.

I did not call Bailey till the next March. Wouldn't have known what to say, because he was not a talkative man and the only thing we really knew how to do together was fish. If I had been older at the time, I'd have figured some excuse to strike up a conversation between seasons. All winter I'd been hoping that he'd know me well enough, in a second season, to trust me with the secret springs. I would have treated them right, Lord knows.

Bailey's wife said that he'd died. It was a short conversation. I wanted to ask for his old steel fly rod but was afraid she'd think me one of those false friends who exploit widows. I just said that I was sorry, and she probably knew I meant it, but if I was tongue-tied then, maybe this will explain.

An Artist with the Fly Rod

Cinquefoil Creek looked sterile where we started our hike, a sluice so narrow that the willows on each bank overlapped in the middle. If anyone but Scotty Chapman had been in the lead, I would have suggested that we look for a better place to fish. But Scotty knows more about Yellowstone National Park's waters than I do. Perhaps he knows more than anyone.

The two of us walked upstream, looping around clumps of charred lodgepole pine. Where the trees stood singly, some had survived the great fires of 1988, and now they dotted the meadow with patches of shade. In this deep-green field, phlox and larkspur sparkled like stars in the Milky Way. We angled up a ridge then, and when its sunburned grass had wiped the dew from our boots, Scotty paused for a breather. He did not like having to do that. Ten years earlier, when he was in his seventies, he had stopped only to capture details for his paintings.

The break from our climb suited me. Scotty is not one to sit around reminiscing, but he is good for a story on the trail.

Scotty Chapman first saw Yellowstone in 1927, after a ten-day drive from Colorado over unpaved roads. The Wyoming headwinds brought his Model T Ford to a shuddering halt sometimes. Sounds like a long journey—until you remember that some of us spend all of our lives searching for the most beautiful place in the world. Scotty found what he was looking for on the first try.

He was "a fishing nut already," he says, and Yellowstone's Firehole River was at its peak in those years. Old Faithful and dozens of other sources of warm water must have created ideal conditions for growth. Trout often reached 3 1/2 pounds, sometimes 5—but these were browns of European origin, too wary for the standard American methods of the time. Most anglers waded downstream, cast wet flies on leaders of stout gut, and caught the smaller trout or none at all. There was not even a fisherman's trail on the banks.

Scotty had read a book on dry-fly fishing by George La Branche, and the Firehole taught the rest of the skills needed for big, selective trout. It was a sport that followed nature's rules. You had to find a hatch of mayflies and a trout rising for them. The heavy browns usually fed under overhanging grass, so you had to sneak up the bank and kneel to cast, sometimes with one leg in the water. You had to convince the trout that your artificial fly was the real thing.

*In 1930, Scotty became a park ranger. In 1937, writer
Ray Bergman visited Yellowstone, and Scotty introduced him
to the Firehole. Bergman wrote that it had "more sizable fish
to the mile than I've ever seen in any other stream," but they
"thumbed their noses at me."*

*Bergman quotes Scotty as asking: "Did you try dry flies
in size 18 and smaller?" The leader had to taper down to 4X,
too—finest silkworm gut generally available, and less
dependable than modern 7X. Bergman wrote that "Scotty is
an artist with the fly rod. . . . I've watched many anglers fish,
but I have never seen anyone else who could so regularly
throw the line so that the fly would float without drag under
any conditions."*

*Scotty and Ray Bergman fished together until at least
1951, when I tagged along on one trip. Many of the photos
Bergman used in his stories show Scotty in his ranger hat—a
tall, athletic angler who happened to resemble another
Montanan named Gary Cooper. If you look closely, there is
something else that you may notice. There are no poses of
angler with captured trout, dead or alive. Scotty does not
care to be seen that way.*

Scotty and I hiked over another rise and downhill to the
basin where Cinquefoil Creek flattened out in meanders. In
this hidden playground, the little stream was all dressed up
like big folks. There were undercuts at the outside of the
bends, shady clumps of grass, and riffles that giggled between
the pools. There were even mats of water buttercup, which is
a plant of fertile waters.

We both strung up our fly rods, but Scotty said that he
would look around for a while before he started. He did not

explain—never does—but I guessed that he was catching the scene for his canvas.

I knotted on a small dry fly. It would look like a beetle to the trout but had little white V-wings that I would be able to see as they drifted under shady banks. Then I worked upstream with a short line, and the brook trout came for the fly but did not take it as well as they usually do. They would materialize below it, watch it for a second, and then splash at it and miss or get hooked lightly.

The problem was a good one to have. We had arrived at the perfect time of the morning—the hour between dawn-cold and noon-hot—and the mayflies were returning to lay their eggs on the water. It was not the kind of fishing that one expects to find on hidden little brook-trout streams. But of course an angler should not get so excited that he starts casting before he takes a look around.

I tied a long, fine tippet to the end of my leader and a sparse size-18 fly to the tippet. By that time the trout were rising as far as we could see up the creek. I slipped into the water and moved upstream, step after cautious step, like a heron, and draped the leader over tufts of grass, hiding it from the fish. When the cast was right, they took the new fly confidently. I put some back and kept the best, 8 or 9 inches long.

Scotty was bored by my heron act before I landed the third trout. He picked up his tackle and rushed upstream, working out line as he went, rod drawing dark loops on blue sky. I walked to the top of a rise and watched.

Above the angler were round golden hills and purple mountains with streaks of old snow in their folds. Those are an amateur's colors—Scotty could tell you the exact pigments.

He was a tall, straight figure against the meadow, fifty years younger with the urge upon him.

The scene from my hilltop was an impressionist sketch—dash of predator, splash of prey. He fished like an osprey, using speed and surprise rather than stealth. I don't know anyone else who can make a fly pounce on trout like that. He did not wade, seldom knelt, but cruised up the bank—false casting, pausing momentarily to drop his fly on likely spots. It was not the Firehole method, but these were not Firehole trout, and they would rise in the second or two before fear overtook hunger. Scotty knew his fish with the intimacy that only a wild predator usually achieves.

By the time I rejoined him, he was cleaning five brook trout between 6 and 10 inches in length. He had taken them "as they came," he said. Fifty years earlier, he had returned big trout to the Firehole, and that was before most people had heard of catch-and-release fishing. He said that he no longer liked to "hot-lip" fish unless he needed them for food.

When I had started following Scotty around the park as a teenager, there were times when I wondered where he was going, but I kept my thoughts to myself except on one hike cross-country through miles of lodgepole tangle that would have dizzied a compass. I said then that I feared we had drifted off course—and I confess that it was a frivolous comment, aimed at getting his reaction.

There was no reaction. Scotty kept on without a word, and in fifteen minutes we hit the shore of a little lake right where we wanted to fish. A goldeneye duck whistled in for a landing, cutting a long silver furrow on the pewter surface, and I promised myself that I would not venture again to tell Scotty Chapman how to find his way around Yellowstone.

He would not say this, but I suppose that nobody else has ever covered as many miles of the park on his own two legs. Not the Sheepeater Indians. (They didn't run patrols.) Not the mountain men. (They didn't last long.) Not today's rangers. (There are committed people among them, but they don't spend the winters on ski patrols.) You could drop Scotty without a map anywhere in Yellowstone's 3,500 square miles and figure that he would hike straight to anywhere else he had a mind to be.

He was Assistant Chief Ranger and fire boss when that was the toughest job in the park. (Scotty would not say this either, but everybody knew it, back then.) Hundreds of firefighters had to be mobilized on short notice. They had to be given tools, food, experienced crew leaders, and quick, clear orders. These were as close to military campaigns as anything in civilian life.

I was a fire guard during some of those summers, and we did not have the resources to put out a sizable fire all at once. Someone had to know where the burn would do more good than harm, keeping the meadows open. On steep, fragile watersheds, however, the flames had to be stopped before they could destroy the trees protecting stream quality. You had to know what you were doing—and do it. You could not duck decisions.

There is a good deal of talk about controlled burns today. With Scotty in charge, we always had controlled burns. I don't suppose that he saw Yellowstone as his biggest canvas. That's just how life turned out.

We were late for lunch by the time we got back to Scotty's ranch, which lies against the northern boundary of Yellowstone. With the exception of near-fatal duty in the Philippines during World War II, nothing had separated him from his park. He had declined transfers and the promotions that would have come with them. I asked him some silly questions over the years, but I never asked if he planned to retire in Florida.

Scotty and his wife, Louise, cooked our trout luncheon. She had shared his commitment since 1932. During the couple's first winter in the park, they lived in an isolated cabin on Soda Butte Creek, and Louise kept the home fire burning, literally. Heating was by woodstove, and the water supply was a spring outside. Scotty was usually away on duty— rounding up the buffalo herd or patrolling for poachers. The patrols were real cross-country work, on nine-foot skis in deep powder, two weeks at a time. "Louise never complained," Scotty says. "I did, but she didn't."

The next winter, Scotty was assigned to the Bechler River cabin, even more remote. Louise left in December to have their first child and came back with baby Bill, in January, on a dog sled. She looks like a model, pretty and fragile.

We sat at the table with afternoon sun streaming through the windows and pulled bones away from the pink, steaming meat of our trout, eating in little bites. We had enough but were not stuffed. And then we talked. I don't remember most of what we said because one casual comment by Scotty got me thinking.

He had been fishing the good spot on Cinquefoil Creek all these years, Scotty said, but he had not shown it to anyone till he took me to it that morning.

I guess I'll be keeping an eye on the place.

An American Original

Vincent C. Marinaro's house was at 600 East Marble Street in Mechanicsburg, Pennsylvania, but he lived on the banks of the Letort Spring Run. At least, he seemed to live there during the summers I knew him, starting in 1971. If we spent an hour or so in the house before fishing, it was because his tackle was stored there. A big winesap tree shaded the back porch, and Vince's rods had been planed from bamboo strips in that small room. Usually we'd take one of the finished rods, or two or three, out of a battered leather case, which, he said, "had been over a lot of iron bridges." I'd hold the screen door open carefully so the tips wouldn't snag. Then we'd cast on the lawn as the sun dropped. Vince would compliment the old tree for setting a crop of apples that would do him and his wife all winter. I'd compliment him on his rods, which was easy. He wouldn't compliment mine, but he would allow that one French rod might get the job done. And then we'd go fishing.

On the banks of the Letort, Vince Marinaro fit as woodcock fit in alder bottoms and brown trout fit under clots of elodea. He moved slowly in his later years, because of a bad hip, so he would take root like a gray-barked hickory stump. I'd thrash my way through a mile of ragweed without seeing a rise—nothing rises in the Letort while the June sun is still hot—and then I'd thrash back, sneezing, and see Vince in the riverbank reeds, rod sticking up like a flowering stem and eyes sharp on the wrinkle of current where a fish would show when its time came. A cigar would be branching out from the corner of his mouth. Probably he did not actually smell like tobacco and bulrushes and limestone mud and the pollen of every tree in the mid-Atlantic, but that's the way my memory of him smells.

The sun would, after a thirty-two-hour day, drop behind the trees and give us a few minutes of evening. The sulphur mayflies would float down the stream, and Vince would get two or three trout, including the best of the evening, which was likely to be about 16 inches long, a little thin, with a pink sheen along the sides and big black spots: the old Letort strain, which always made Vince happy. In the near-dark, his rod would flicker a few more times, throwing line back high over the greenery, dropping "puddle casts," and perhaps bowing to another fish as a pair of late mallards whistled up the river.

Vince won't be on the Letort's bank again but I haven't a proper obituary in me. He was a private and compartmented person. He liked to talk about what was under a few of the lids, and I made no attempt to open the others, which may be one reason why we got along.

Some scholar may do more research. What I have is a few years of memories that are sharp but disconnected, like film sequences without a script.

Marinaro's Books

Vince did not write two important books just because he happened to be in the right place at the right time, though of course that helped. He did everything well, if he was interested in it, and worked at it till it was perfect. His second book (*In the Ring of the Rise*) had pictures of rising brown trout that seemed impossibly good, and if you didn't know him, you would have to wonder what tricks he pulled. You might suspect that his photographs were akin to others the outdoor magazines used to run, with fish performing faked leaps. But Marinaro's pictures were as uncompromising as the man behind the camera. He set up blinds along the banks of the upper Letort and ran countless rolls of film through his old Leica with the reflex housing. His subjects were all stream-bred trout, unconfined and rising to natural insects. The river was open to fishing, so other anglers cast to those fish. If you have tried to see Letort trout, let alone photograph them, you will understand the dimensions of the problem.

Vince's reputation, however, had been made by *A Modern Dry-Fly Code,* first published in 1950. The worth of a book must be a matter of opinion, but I will not be alone in suggesting that this was the first great American innovative work in its field. That field is fishing with flies that imitate natural insects. There had, of course, been other good fishing books in America by 1950, and there had even been two good ones on imitative flies by Preston Jennings and Art Flick. This, however, was a subject on which Vince and I did not agree, as I discovered when he went through a manuscript of mine in the mid-1970s. Jennings and Flick were honest and sound; they knew their trout and their natural insects; and, in my view, both men tied splendid floating flies in the traditional design.

Vince, however, had a low opinion of the Halfordian (and Catskill) dry fly. For him there were no good traditional dry flies. In *A Modern Dry-Fly Code*, he reproached G. E. M. Skues for not having "emancipated" the dry fly as he did the wet. The Halfordian dry fly was, he thought, no more than a maladapted wet fly—so you can imagine his opinion of Americans who were using it late in the twentieth century.

Marinaro rethought the design of the dry fly from head to tail, and the *Code* provided clear alternatives. But I want to be precise on what Vince did and did not do. He proposed more successful new dry-fly designs than any writer before him. It is fair to say that he did for the dry fly what Skues had done for the wet. At the same time, the *Code* was squarely within the great tradition of fly fishing. It is impossible to think of the book being written in any language but English. (This is my opinion—not one that I recall discussing with the author.)

As between the English and American schools, Vince clearly found more guidance in the former. He collected English books, flies, and tying materials. But within the great tradition he was an entrepreneur, not an adapter.

Originality has its costs. Americans were waiting for the great American novel long after it had been published, and the *Code* was similarly ahead of its time. A mutual friend told me that the first edition was remaindered in Philadelphia for a dollar a copy. A few years later, before the new edition of 1970, the 1950 edition was sold for a hundred times the remaindered price—which, of course, did nothing for the author's bank account but must have made him feel better. In the time I knew him, Vince was wary of the angling public, and of other authors, too. Perhaps the book's slow reception left a mark on him, but someone who knew him in the 1950s would have to address that.

For me, at least, 1950 is the watershed in American fly fishing. In the years since, other good books have appeared, and vast (but still incomplete) work has been done on American trout-stream insects. There could have been no better model than Marinaro. He was a lawyer, and the *Code* made good case law: a treatise that could be argued for decades before the court of anglers without proving flawed. Vince claimed nothing that he had not done, repeatedly. There were no evasive generalities to fail scrutiny. Sources got credit. If you open the book today for the first time, you will have no feeling that you are reading something dated. Everything in it works, and always will.

INNOVATIONS

Perhaps Vince (like Skues) left a list somewhere of contributions that he considered important. If so, I have not seen it, but here are some of the innovations in the *Code*:

- Divided tails, which help in persuading a winged fly to land and float upright. As far as I know, Vince was the first who thoroughly understood what tails could do for a dry fly.

- The "thorax" tie, with hackles wound well back from the eye of the hook and a thorax formed in front of them. (Since 1950, other mayfly designs have adopted this principle.)
- An arrangement of hackles designed to make the fly float flat or slightly nose-down on the water, like a real mayfly. (Marinaro's original design is still used but is difficult to tie, and many successors use easier designs.)
- A series of terrestrial flies, including an ant with hackle in the center of the body, a jassid, an innovative grasshopper, and a beetle. I'm not clear as to precedents for all of these flies, but it is certain that Marinaro played a major role and that his book gave many American anglers the idea of fishing with terrestrials.

OTHER WRITING

Vince did a lifetime of angling research, but I am aware of only the following published writing: two books already mentioned, four articles for *Outdoor Life,* and the foreword to my 1982 book. Everything he did will get attention from historians, so I should say a little more about the foreword, which taught me some things about him.

Most of his contributions had already been made—via the *Code*—before he saw my manuscript on the design of trout flies. Of the thirty-eight designs I listed, three were totally Marinaro and seven others had been influenced by him. Even that count excludes the impact of his V-tail, which helps a dry fly land upright.

To my surprise, Vince had little to say about the flies I described in *What the Trout Said.* He must have disagreed on some points (like the usefulness of the traditional dry fly), but not on the facts. On style, he had suggestions. "Never give readers more than one thought per page," he counseled. Several times he opined that too much was packed into a passage. The chapter he seemed to like best was the first, on the importance of listening to trout. (I changed the other chapters to be more like the first.)

Vince clearly liked the idea of assessing a wide range of designs. (He had not done so, nor had he used the term *design,* though he was our greatest fly designer.)

Now, Vince could be counted on for a brutally frank critique, which was all I had sought, but his reaction encouraged me to ask him for a foreword. He thought about this for months, and worried aloud. I suppose he knew that his blessing would be important to me, though we did not discuss that. What he said was that he had been asked to read a number of manuscripts over the years and had announced a policy of writing no forewords. If he did one now, he would make other authors unhappy. (It was the only time I heard him express concern about stepping on toes.) But he said he'd think about the foreword, and when he decided to go ahead, he did so with a generosity that was also typical.

Vince seemed to feel a continuing responsibility for the book after its publication, and when we went fishing, he would give me new ideas and bits of information. On our last trip of 1985, he told me of his surprise in finding a 1966 book (by W. H. Lawrie) that used the term *design* and analyzed traditional wet flies in terms of their design. That discovery gave me a chance to rectify an oversight before my second edition.

I suppose that, if he had not chosen to put so much of his intellectual energy into fishing, lawyer Marinaro would have enjoyed being a judge.

GOOD RODS

Of the bamboo rods I had handled, those made by Vince were best. They started, at the long end, with a double-handed salmon rod. His personal favorite for trout was a 9-foot, 3-piece, 4-ounce rod for a 6-weight line. (He was unable to wade much because of his hip, so he wanted a long rod to clear the bank foliage.)

My favorites were the 8- and 7½-footers, which weighed about two-thirds as much as my own rods—and cast better. Then there was the 6-foot rod for a 3-weight line. It weighed, Vince said, just less than an ounce, and it was a real fishing tool, not a toy like the old Leonard "Baby Catskill." We proved this point with long, easy casts under the old apple tree.

The tapers appealed to me even more than the weights. Correct rod tapers, for Marinaro, were not a matter of individual preference: There were specific tasks that the rod had to perform well or it was simply a bad rod. But if you have read *In the Ring of the Rise,* you will know that Vince was uncharacteristically evasive about dimensions. If asked, he would say that he did not want anyone making bad rods from his convex tapers, and the other tricks of the trade were as important as dimensions in thousandths of an inch.

I know that Vince was unhappy because no rod maker with an adequate milling machine had ever asked him to put rods in production. (He used planing forms only because he had no alternative.) He would not sell individual rods because he didn't want "to sell a ten-thousand-dollar design for a thousand dollars." It was one subject on which we did argue. I urged him to put what he knew about rod building in a book, because it was getting to be difficult enough to make bamboo rods that would hold their own against the synthetics, and he should not let the best designs disappear without a ripple. Vince did not write the book, and as far as I know, his tapers and notes are not available to rod builders.

PASSION

Fly fishing has been called an intellectual passion, and there are few people who have proved it more thoroughly than Vince Marinaro. He figured out how to braid horsehair lines, using an authentic gadget he found at a flea market. He reconstructed the old British North Country flies, taking pains to find authentic materials. (Who else had dotterel feathers?) But Vince's passions had nothing to do with price or prestige. I heard him express admiration for a few books, a rooster's cape with silver-colored hackles, some old Hardy silk lines, one or two Partridge hooks, good double-barreled shotguns, a rod by Tom Maxwell, and a pair of hackle pliers. "That's the only good pair of hackle pliers I ever saw," he said.

The list of things Marinaro did not like was longer but expressed with equal frankness, if anyone asked. He held conventional wisdom in such disregard that some interlocutors found him unsettling. In addition to Halfordian flies, he disliked:

- Many prestigious bamboo rods, especially if they had stiff butts or soft middles.
- Overwhelming trout with modern technology. Vince got so that he would not willingly walk into a shop where he had to look at graphite rods, which he found lacking in soul, repulsive, "almost slimy." But, at an earlier stage, he once admitted that an Orvis 9-foot, 3-inch graphite rod for a 6-weight line cast well.

- Trout streams (or grouse covers) with lots of people in them.
- Writers who attract crowds by publicizing individual streams. (But, for friends who could keep their mouths shut, he was generous in sharing knowledge of the best streams in Pennsylvania.)
- Many fishing books. When I praised a well-known author and fly tyer, Vince said that he had visited the Au Sable River in Michigan with this man and found him "fishing the water" (casting at random) when there were visible rises to cover. I did not know enough to press the point, but I wondered whether the other angler could see rising trout as well as Marinaro, whose eyesight was keen till the end.

The *Code* made clear which kind of fishing Vince liked best. He was not, however, a dry-fly purist. On one of our last trips to the Letort, he experimented with old-fashioned wet flies on little double hooks. I don't recall seeing him nymph fishing. One day, though, I was fishing a little beetle upstream and wet, just like a Skues-style nymph, and Vince invited me to try two small Letort fish that had refused his dry fly. He seemed delighted when they took the beetle. I think he enjoyed filing that away as another angling problem solved.

It was easy to know when Vince was not pleased. You can be sure that I did not "pollute the water" (his term) with rods of synthetic materials when we went fishing together.

MYSTERIES OF LIFE

Among the subjects on which I sought Vince's advice was the relationship between women and field sports. He told me that his wife—he called her "Mom"—had gone fishing with him exactly once, early in their marriage. But she had never objected when, several evenings a week, he rushed home from the office and out to the Letort. Then when he returned late at night, she always had a good meal ready for him and any friend he brought along (and to this I can testify). She was "a real fisherman's wife," he said, and when she died in 1978, he floated lower in the water.

About then I started driving up to Mechanicsburg on Friday evenings, occasionally, and sleeping over so that we could make a start before dawn for the best of summer hatches. Vince had introduced me—and the country as a whole—to the *Tricorythodes* mayflies.

Throughout America, the Trico hatch must now be the most important we have—and we did not know it existed till Marinaro's article of July 1969 in *Outdoor Life*. It was the angling equivalent of Columbus's discovery in 1492.

Vince took pleasure in the Tricos right through the summer of 1985, which was his last. In July he showed me an original Trico spinner design that he considered the best ever. He also explained exactly how to fish for trout "gulping" the tiny flies—and why a bamboo rod worked better than anything else for the purpose.

After the hatch we'd go back to 600 East Marble Street for lunch. Vince never did let me stop at a restaurant, and his cooking was still good, but the old winesap tree hadn't been pruned, and windfalls covered the backyard. But there was still a swath of mowed grass for casting. Inside the house there were paths between piles of waders, long-handled wading nets, fishing bags, rod cases, guns, and fly-tying gear. On the wall was a sconce with three unburned candles drooping in the heat: one bending like rod on the backcast, one near surrender, and one limp. Near this were a Limestoner award and a plaque from the Theodore Gordon Flyfishers for Vince's contribution to the literature. He must have felt good about these awards, but he'd have been embarrassed if I'd mentioned them.

It was, however, open season on his fly boxes, and I could prowl through them as much as I liked. Then we'd scout some trout streams, desultorily, and some bird coverts, seriously. Vince would shake his head when he saw the traffic jam on the Yellow Breeches. For the last couple of years, he hadn't been willing to face that horde of anglers even to fish the white fly, which he considered a better spectacle than the Tricos. He had worked hard to get fish-for-fun regulations on some of the limestone spring creeks, but now he preferred to fish elsewhere—without so many trout, perhaps, but also without so many anglers. Besides, he said, he liked to eat a trout now and then.

He got more pleasure from the doves. After opening day in September, the hunting would get as crowded as the fishing, but in July the birds still whistled around, a reminder of the times when you could get two cock pheasants in any cornfield and Cedar Run still had trout in it.

To my knowledge, Vince did not write about hunting, but he enjoyed it as much as fishing: Indeed, he seemed to draw no line between the two. By the time I knew him, however, he walked so slowly that my dog (a German shorthaired pointer) found our hunting trips puzzling. I remember creeping through one woodcock covert, full of good smells, while Trooper ran back and forth in front of us, and back and forth, and back and forth. No covert has ever been covered like that one.

On a dove stand, however, legs did not matter much, and Vince was a good shot with his vintage Remington Model 32. It had a Miller single trigger for instant, effective barrel selection, and it seemed typical of him to have worked out that problem too.

But mostly we drove around slowly, revisiting Vince's favorite streams and coverts, and he shot every dove that crossed our path—with his forefinger.

Any shotgunner would have enjoyed calculating the leads. An incoming dove would slip by at that peculiar angle that makes shots tricky and Vince would go "Bang!", cackling like a nine-year-old slaying dinosaurs. He spotted more doves than I did. "Bang!" he'd exult, wiping my eye. "You sure missed that one!" It's my other favorite memory.

Vince crossed his last iron bridge on March 2, 1986.

Lunch by the Stream

Curt Collins is a natural for next summer's Montana movie. Between beard and straw hat, his skin is oil-tanned leather, and he looks as if he could row against the current because that's what he does, 180 days a year. On his chest, furthermore, hangs a "guide's necklace" loaded with problem-solving equipment—the 1990s equivalent of a .45-caliber shell belt. I spotted an emergency capsule of flies, spools of leader material, flotants for both regular dry flies and those with duck-butt feathers, containers of split shot and lead sleeves, a leader clipper, and two medical forceps, which are used to remove hooks from trout. Curt mentioned that the forceps were also his "best cooking tools" for streamside lunches. I nodded as if I knew what he was talking about.

Curt spends the fishing season in Fort Smith—a boom town built by a single natural resource, like so many others in the High West. In this case, however, the resource is aquatic insects, which nourish big wild trout, which in turn attract fly fishers from all over the world. The Bighorn is a destination river.

It is not an easy river to read, however. The vast solar energy in the Bighorn's depths is hidden by a big, calm surface, which makes the stream a good match for Curt Collins. When the tailwater fishery became legal in 1981, he was the first in line for an outfitter's license.

Our days on the stream started early, with hordes of little Tricos—mayflies of the genus *Tricorythodes*—falling spent on the water. At dusk there was a caddisfly hatch, also heavy. In between, I fished exactly where Curt told me with a pair of his soft-hackle sow bugs. The Bighorn's bragging trout are mostly rainbows, he said, and his boat's best for the year was an 11-pounder. I'd have bragged about my 21-inch brown.

Our double shifts on the river were separated by a meal that Curt called lunch, though it looked more like Sunday dinner. When the trout stopped feeding, we started.

First thing out of our boat was a folding table with red-checked tablecloth and stools. Then came two propane barbecue grills and tableware, which included wineglasses. From a cooler the size of a life raft, Curt produced a bottle of cold white wine, two cheeses, a summer sausage, strawberries, green grapes, chunks of melon, loaves of bread, a whole pie—and the main course.

Every real cook likes to see his food appreciated, so I did the appreciating while Curt did the work. On one of the grills, he piled baked potatoes and ears of sweet corn, each precooked, buttered, and wrapped in aluminum foil. He closed the lid of that grill. On the other, he melted a smidgen of margarine, or perhaps two smidgens, in a foil tray. When the fat was bubbling, several handfuls of big shrimp went in the tray, then filets of orange roughy, and finally a few shakes of lemon pepper, garlic pepper, and garlic powder. He manipulated the hot foil with his quick-draw forceps.

The fish and shrimp were not overcooked. The potatoes were not undercooked. The pan sauce was just right. This is the truth, uninfluenced by September sunshine, the rustle of cottonwood trees, and the smell of buffaloberries ripening in the sun. After lunch I picked a gallon of the berries before Curt reported that trout were moving into the riffles.

Here and there in my travels, there have been a few other cooks who could put such meals together. None of them did it on portable grills, in between pulling oars and rigging lead sleeves for sow bugs.

That evening, while watching Curt Collins prepare the next day's lunch, I deduced that the man runs on solar power, like his river. He recharges himself every day, and the energy keeps him going far into the night.

"You have to start with good raw materials," Curt said. He boiled homegrown corn on the cob for seven minutes, then let it sit in the water for a few more. He baked potatoes in the microwave oven, sliced them, layered them with uncooked sliced onions, and sprinkled with seasoning salt and garlic powder. He simmered Cornish hens and stuffed them. Each dish was wrapped separately in buttered foil. While he was preparing the acorn squash with buffaloberry jam, I dozed off and missed seeing him get the trimmings ready, but all of them emerged from his cooler the next afternoon.

Fishing and cooking are both ways of living with nature, when you think about it, and one works up an appetite for the other. You are a predator, Mr. or Ms. Fly Fisher. Might as well behave like one. Even trout pause for digestion when they have caught enough of their prey.

The First Time

"It's crying time again," sang Anna. "You're gonna leave me. I can see that faraway look in your eyes." Translation: My wife was hooshing me out of the house so that she could hold a meeting of her women's investment club without free advice.

By the time I reached the Madison River, it was late morning, but I would have taken time to coach the two women in clean waders and vests with empty pockets—the angling-school equivalent of an academic cap and gown. The newcomers were making thirty-foot casts in shallow water right by the parking place. When I asked what they were using, one of the women said "Prince Nymph" without looking at me, so I moved on.

A quarter mile upstream, *Baetis* duns were hatching and blowing away in a gale that discouraged even swallows. Then the wind dropped—preparing to change directions—and the riffle above a good pool was covered by tiny sailboats tempest-tossed. Five fish began feeding on the surface, and I caught two of them on a size-20 emerger. One trout was a rainbow as long as my forearm, but still thin from spawning. The other was a fat young silvery brown that jumped twice and vibrated in my hand as I removed the hook.

I released both. Fresh fish would be welcome on the table, but trout from the Madison River do not taste as good as they look.

The wind came back hard under my visor, so I turned around and splashed downstream to the truck. The two women were still where I had left them, casting ten yards and wondering what to do next. (Wading takes longer to learn than casting, if you have not grown up on mossy rocks.)

When the scream came I ran to help, trained husband that I am, but the emergency was a trout, young splashing brown like mine but caught by a maiden's personal Prince. Scream turned to laugh as the fish came in at high speed and dangled in the air, swinging back and forth while the angler tried to catch it in her bare hand. She did, too. Grasped it firmly, sort of, removed the hook, turned her prey loose, and kept on screaming while cliffs on the far bank screamed back echoes.

"That's my first trout," she said.

PART TWO

Running Water

Faith in a Fly

*Y*ou *kept the faith through cold months, tying flies by the fire. You knew that the forsythia would bloom and the tulip trees would send out buds like ducks' bills. You knew that the sun would pull up mayflies, the mayflies would pull up trout, and the trout would pull you into running water. None of you are sun lovers, exactly. Fish and flies are usually most active under mild gray skies and so are you, but in spring you need a burst of energy and a surge of life. You may not catch many trout, with so much competition from nature. But you will be awake.*

Sources

I know a stream that no one else has fished. An Indian would hardly have bothered with its little trout, not when he saw the moose tracks all around, and an angler in step with the times would ignore a thin blue line on the map. Neither big-game hunter nor big-water angler would have the right equipment, anyhow. Flint arrowhead could not hit a shadow fish. Neoprene waders would not survive the talus slope.

My discovery came when I was hunting grouse in yellow aspens one fall and stumbled into water deep enough to soak my socks. The creek was hidden by overhanging grass and so cold that it made me jump. I was not sure that my secret stream was big enough to hold trout and did not try to find them, not just then. With winter around the corner, there was no need to clutter my imagination with the facts.

Next summer, however, when rivers down in the civilized world were growing pondweed, I climbed back up the mountain and explored what turned out to be a real spring creek, tiny but full to the brim. In its first pool, there was a puff of silt—not much of a sign, but enough to show that a fish had spooked.

An arrow shot upstream, I cast a fly where the trunk of a fallen spruce backed up dark water. What happened next did not look like a fish. It looked like an iris opening its flower, blossoming without motion, growing closer to the sun. I struck when the petals came to resemble fins, but the trout had not reached full bloom. It folded itself back into shadow.

For the next pool, I switched to a beetle fly because an eminent scientist had concluded that God is inordinately fond of beetles. A fish took the fly, rasped my tippet on a boulder, but could not break off. When the trout slid onto my hand, it reached from fingertip to cuff button and shivered with the colors of spruces and sunsets. I thought that God must be inordinately fond of brook trout, too.

A Place at Dawn

Our nation's capital is not where you might expect to find trout fishermen. It steeps in a region of humid air, dry rivers, low altitude, and high confusion. Most of the week, Washington frets about anything except fish. Put yourself in this situation, however, and tell me what you would like to do on the weekend.

People are the same here. There must be somebody in the city who doesn't want to go fishing—perhaps even several such people, though I haven't met them. The difference is that upscale young professionals don't start with worms and sunfish, like the rest of us. When they've bought their cathedral-ceilinged town-houses and BMWs, they want fly rods. Then they go to fishing schools and start taking up space on my favorite streams.

The change is for the good—I guess. We need the new-comers to vote for running water and care for it. It's just that they care so unanimously, every Saturday. If I wanted a social gathering, I'd go to a party—if there were anybody left in town to give parties.

Shall I tell you of a secret stream which, the biologists say, is underfished? Well, there are a few hallucinating biologists, but the underfished stream is halfway between Novosibirsk and Vladivostok. It has carp.

There is, however, a secret place in time. When the moon has set and the rising sun is a deep red, my stream will be there, still secret, under the river mists of next summer's dawns.

Company is nice on long predawn trips, so a hard-driving buddy and I teamed up a couple of times last year, and getting there was half the fun. Maybe more than half: H.D. makes great conversation. He didn't take all that long to wake up, either, considering that this was three hours earlier than usual, and Lord knows he has a right to be tired. We rummaged around for his gear, then drove to the Quik & Dirty for a breakfast of home-fried cholesterol, which improved his attitude, and strong coffee got the talk flowing, among other things. Coffee is a diuretic. Translation: it required a stop just down the road. By that time the caffeine was wearing off, so we tanked up again. Made it to the river after just one more stop.

I was only half right about the BMWs. The other half was four-wheel-drive trucks. When we got to the bridge, their 7.2-liter V-8s were already subduing the puddles in the parking pullout.

That's when I knew we were late: Your huddled masses yearning to breathe free never show up till the fishing is over. The sun was throwing sharp shadows as I broke a record for the thousand-yard dash in chest waders. Somewhere upstream there had to be a trout working overtime.

H.D. was running low on fuel by now, so he fished near the car, and he said, later, that he'd had a good time, even if the trout didn't appreciate the sacrifices he'd made for them.

Those trips got us out of the town, all right, but they didn't get the town out of us. So now, having run out of victims, I follow another rhythm. Funny how many years it took to hear. The streams were simple enough to locate, but it wasn't easy to find the dawn.

Listen to the ghosts. They move before the east begins to turn light on a summer morning. First to appear are those you don't like: ghosts of in-baskets past, present, and future. Whether you like Washington or not—and I don't—you have to admit that people there work hard, and then worry about not working more. An old college coach used to say that every hour of sleep before midnight was worth two afterward. I guess he knew that the ghost of work unfinished likes to rouse a fellow in the small hours.

You could go to work instead of fishing. You could put a pillow over your head and return to a sweaty sleep. Alternatively, you could call up a better variety of ghost. I tune in the Pennsylvania limestone country, back when there was a cock pheasant crowing in each fallow field. I see spring creeks running full, without Styrofoam cups bobbing around. The ghost of Vince Marinaro is moving upstream at first light with his cigar laying down a fog.

This kind of ghost is tuned to the right frequency, unlike my clock radio with its bad news. The distance between bed and car is short, and getting out of town is easy, too: All roads run from Washington, and no one is on them at this hour except me, a raccoon flashing his eyes just up the street, and a fox wafting across the beam of my headlights. Let's not count the purée of parkway possum; possums should never attempt to waft. But except for them, the ghosts are comforting. Like other urban areas, Washington is a wildlife refuge, up to a point. You wouldn't expect grizzly bears.

I am awake. Not high, but not about to doze off, either. As a kid in Montana, one of my great discoveries was that coffee made the sun rise. Then, as an older kid in Washington, I discovered that what goes up must come down. I don't want to be down when the fish start rising.

There are ghosts to look for in the limestone country. Once it was covered with passenger pigeons, and there were elk, even bison. When I came on scene in the 1960s, buffalo were scarce but there were still so many pheasants, quail, and rabbits that we could hunt any old way and get enough for Sunday dinner.

Now I slow, roll down the window, and let a soft breeze wash me clean of town. At the same time I breakfast on Proper's Patented Silent Sandwiches, which are made of leftover waffles. They will sustain me through a day's fishing without lunch, if it comes to that. They will also let me drive, eat, and listen for cackling pheasants at the same time.

I do not hear any. The limestone abundance is still there, but now it is expressed in grackles and starlings, which are surly before sunrise, like upscale young professionals.

On a side road closer to the Letort Spring Run, rabbits reappear in force. One of them seems to be playing with a gray squirrel or—more likely—discussing who's in charge around here. A woodchuck waddles for his hole when I slow down. (He looks like me in waders.) These are animals that thrive either on the farms or in suburbia, and the limestone country today is a mixture. New houses with new trucks are just behind the fog. The old red-roofed barns are still here, but the farmhouses are rented. The farmers are in Florida.

At this time between night and day, though, the town called York Springs looks about as it used to. (The new money wants country, not old towns.) There is Bosserman's Grocery, Ma's Kitchen, big old brick houses, and little white frame houses with old log cabins behind the new siding. And just on the other side of the Appalachian Trail, there is a spring where I will drink on the way home. It runs from hills where a few American chestnuts live long enough to produce a sweet harvest.

When I reach the stream, mist still hangs thick over cool, clear water. This is progress: Before the new sewage plant, the Letort was too polluted for mayflies or salmonids. Now the trout gorge on Tricos from July through September.

More good news: The Tricos are not hatching yet. Tricos are very small mayflies of the genus *Tricorythodes* that emerge in very large numbers—but sometimes at night, when the weather is especially hot and sultry. I rush to sneak off before the crowd shows up and somebody wants to follow me.

There is another reason for furtiveness: women, who arrive in the front of BMWs and the back seat of trucks. Each woman is accompanied by a man, and each wears a safari shirt, new cap, and fishing vest. This too is progress. When women defend trout streams, politicians listen. And besides, the newcomers look good even in waders.

The problem is that I do not measure up. The real me is hidden by a sweaty visor, a pair of flip-up sunglasses, a shirt that gave at the office, and Army-surplus pants with one pocket converted to a patch. My image began to worry me when I noticed the girls scooting back toward their boyfriends as I stalked the banks. Then I saw how the hero dressed in a movie called *Revenge of the Nerds,* and everything became clear: I thought I was looking for trout, but the women thought I wanted revenge.

This will change. Khaki paraphernalia comes on sale in September, and next summer, Ma'am, you will see a new man on the Spring Run. You are a civilizing influence.

Upstream, the spoor of the anglers dwindles quickly. They can't drive here, and the banks are rank with thistles, sedges, and wild snapdragons. Underfoot, muskrat holes drop suddenly to four feet of spring water. This is not like a brook-trout stream in the woods—but it's wild.

A pheasant agrees. I hear the first of the day crowing, down in that jungle somewhere, then a second replying from upstream. They complete the exorcising of Washington.

Two big watersnakes have crawled out on a jumble of logs blocking a side current, reminding me that last week I was casting to a decent brown trout when a snake grabbed it by the tail. The trout got loose, but not till all three of us argued for a while. Now, while snakes glare at me, I notice the faintest movement at the edge of a scum above the logs. A minute later the ripple comes again. I cast over the logs and a trout takes innocently. It could tangle me, if it knew what to do, but it comes flapping over the logs before it figures out what happened. It is only a stocked rainbow with stubby fins.

Then a real mayfly drifts safely downstream, so I turn around and squint toward light in the east, seeing more: little disembodied wings glinting in the air like sunbeams. Tricos. The trout will tell me what to do from now on.

This stream is supposed to be difficult to fish—and it is, after the trout have filled their bellies. But now they are hungry, and humid air dims the low sun enough to let me cast from a comfortable twenty or thirty feet. It is a place to renew my confidence that I am sometimes smarter than a fish.

Or at least smarter than stocked rainbows. The hatchery browns aren't much more clever: They have been in the stream over winter, but they come from a strain bred to tolerate crowding. These are not the ghosts I seek.

There. A real trout rises at last, but he lives beneath overhanging clumps of vegetation. The fly must land in the inches between two grassy traps, then float under others.

When everything works, the fish takes, pulls harder than the rest, but comes to the net. This is a wild brown with fins like a butterfly's wings and a bright rim of sunrise-red on the adipose.

Back at the parking spot, a fishing school is going on, and some of those athletes can throw a fly ninety feet. Reminds me that I've been meaning to learn how to cast one of these days. Meanwhile, I try to sneak into the old moss-colored station wagon. It's moss-colored because there is moss growing on it. (There is no truth, however, to the story that I forgot a woodcock under the seat; I don't get enough woodcock to forget one. Perhaps a silent sandwich did sneak off and hide.) Next season, Ma'am, you will see me in a new metallic-khaki four-wheel-drive, capable of fording the worst humidity this country's got. I'll still be evasive about the fishing, though. It's not a secret, exactly, but I'd just as soon not spread the word that real trout are in here. Besides, you might laugh if I tried to explain about an old place upstream between moon and sun.

Something Old, Something New

The old-timer started me fly fishing backward. He was the only angler I knew who fished upstream with a traditional winged wet fly, and the one who could "catch trout where there weren't any trout," as another angler put it.

In the seasons since then, I have still seen no other American using the up-and-wet method. Maybe it seems outmoded to a generation that grew up with sink-tip lines, split shot, and strike indicators. This old way of fishing does not even require fly flotants and stiff rods, which came along in the next-to-last wave of technology. Our ancestors could have fished the upstream wet fly 500 years ago and probably did, though the instructions they left behind are open to interpretation.

My personal learning disability was a notion that wet flies were for innocent trout. The usual way of fishing them was to cast toward the far bank, more or less, and let the line swing in an arc down and across the stream. The pull of the current kept the line tight, making it relatively easy to hook the fish. They might even hook themselves. The across-and-down method was relaxing, and under the right conditions it worked, but it was not for educated trout under a bright sun.

The upstream wet-fly method is more closely related to dry-fly fishing. The best way to learn, in fact, is to start with a dry fly on fast water—but leave the flotant off. Make short casts upstream, or up and slightly across, and strip in line as the fly sinks and drifts toward you. Keep it as free as possible of unnatural movement. Trout will, however, tolerate sightly more drag in a sunken fly than in a floater.

The hardest part is striking. Rising trout may be visible if the fly is barely under the surface, but with experience you will want to fish deeper, and then you will see no splash from the fish, no twitch of the leader. For a visual clue, try the old method: two or three flies on your leader, top dropper flirting with the surface film. Look on it as a strike indicator with a hook. In Britain and Ireland, where anglers still commonly use more than one wet fly at a time, the top dropper is called a "bob fly"—bobber with a bite.

Somebody has written that trout prefer to feed either on the bottom of the stream or at the surface. Let us give thanks for such advice, which has created a sort of private fishing preserve for midwater flies.

There are no miracle methods, mind you—just ways that work when conditions are right. They were not quite right last year on the Talking Rocks Branch in the Virginia

Appalachians. The winter had been dry and the water was already low in May, but I fished up-and-wet anyhow. The old method just seemed to fit the season, what with leaf mold steaming on the banks and dogwoods blooming in a dark forest.

My bamboo rod was soft, by modern standards, and it presented the fly without drying it. I let it hang in the current below me, after most drifts, and then used a single false cast or none at all. Fly entered water twenty feet or so upstream, and the current pushed it toward me, helping to put a little slack in the tippet, while a high rod kept most of the line off the surface, reducing drag.

The old fly dawdled past sunken logs and shadowy caves, facets of the wing catching stray sunbeams. My casting arm had an easy job but my brain worked as hard as it ever does, willing the fly to wink out. Sometimes, when the sun's angle was right, the whole show was visible. Native brook trout appeared from nowhere, drawn but cautious—instants at the incandescent core of fishing.

Three or four small fish took the fly in the first quarter mile. They were hungry, alive, and spooky, like me. Thunder grumbled from the mountains, the faintest of upstream breezes ruffled the hair on the back of my neck, and the talking rocks sounded more and more human as I worked upstream.

The rocks must have formed a single flat boulder once, but the stream had broken it in half and eroded the fracture to an echo chamber, crosswise to the current. In that voice box, the waves muttered words that I was too clever to understand. Ten feet upstream from the rocks, however, where the stream divided, a rising fish sent me a clear message. Two vigorous false casts flicked the water out of the fly's wing. The line fell across the rocks and the fly dropped onto the V of current, floating. A heavy brook trout sidled over and took confidently.

The upstream fly works both ways, as you see. If you find a fish feeding on the surface, you can convert from wet to dry instantly. And on that day in the Appalachians, the best trout came to a fly drifting sodden in the surface film.

By late June, I was back home in the Rockies, where summer comes late. Indian Creek was clear but high, and a fisherman hiking out said that he had done no good. My weighted nymph did no good either, so I tied on a wet fly, fished it upstream without faith, and hooked three rainbows in the first pool. One of them was big for the stream. In the next few hundred yards, rainbows came to the fly in every decent pocket, and brook trout responded in the slower water under the banks.

Rainbows are the most aggressive of trout, and brook trout are almost as greedy, though not as fast. Browns are more likely to insist on a fly resembling their food of the moment—and yet the upstream wet fly evolved to catch brown trout in Europe.

By August in Montana, the runoff was long past, the sun was hot, and we could almost hear the grass growing. My companion was an excellent angler who had just caught some difficult trout in a weedy spring creek, so I took him to Canyon Creek for a change of pace. There was another reason, too. My wife had ordered five brook trout, which happen to reach peak flavor in early August, at least in my part of the world.

Canyon Creek's bottom consists of one boulder after another—each of which seems to shelter a trout—so my friend tied on a stonefly nymph. It seemed like an obvious choice to both of us.

I hiked a mile farther and worked upstream with a wet fly, just because fishing it was a pleasure. The brook trout turned out to be moody—never a surprise. The rainbow trout, on the other hand, were determined not to let my fly hover in vain. They chewed off the hackle, then the body, and continued to take the white wing. I did not strike when I could identify a rainbow in time, but even so, at least twenty had to be released from a barbless hook before enough brook trout volunteered for dinner.

My friend was honest as well as competent, and he reported that his nymph had caught one fish only—a rainbow. Neither of us could understand why the trout had passed up a realistic modern fly in favor of an antique.

Maybe this old method was simply the only artifice that had never been tried on Canyon Creek's trout.

Maybe the fish saw something in the fly that was invisible to us humans.

Maybe we should accept gifts without asking reasons.

The Best Trout
Stream in the World

The best stream is the one with the most trout, and my eleven-year-old brooks no doubts. Doesn't everyone fish here? Well, they would if they had any sense.

Scotty wades into Henrietta Creek, tucks the butt of my fly rod under the cuff of his shirt, and casts (sort of) where riffle enters pool, or where Henrietta stops her chatter under a dark bank. Drag is no problem because Scotty's casts have plenty of slack in them, and when the fly's white wings float in just the right place—the place where I have been trying to draw an X on the water and show it to my boy—something usually happens. If Scotty does not notice, I yelp. He has learned to strike at yelp as well as splash.

Little brook trout are the fastest, and Scotty misses many of them. Bigger fish, mostly rainbows, are easier. The browns are rarely interested, but the native cutthroats inhale the fly and won't let it go, even when Scotty pauses to argue that this time I am surely imagining the rise.

There is something wayward about a child catching foot-long cutthroats on a dry fly and releasing them. He ought to be snaffling 6-inch brookies on a worm and carrying them to his mom in a fern-lined creel, but he's tall enough to sneak books off the adult shelves. Trout-fishing literature and certain other fantasies should be kept away from minors.

Scotty will discover later that the best stream is the one with the most *big* trout, and he will float a river with so many of them that the skipper runs a covert operation, as if he were smuggling diamonds. Scotty will slither through the willows, peer down, and watch the molecules resolve into a trout so large that he will (temporarily) forget the other things teenagers think about. He may even catch a fish; I did when I was his age. Fishermen never forget such trout, and biologists never do. Biologists, however, are required to be objective, which means measuring the fish and keeping records.

Biomass can be measured. It is most concentrated in supermarkets and after that, usually, in big even-tempered rivers that flow from the depths of reservoirs. Such streams are not quite natural and not quite beautiful, but they are sublime—super natural, in the words of a Canadian advertising slogan.

Edward R. Hewitt's most-cited opinion is that the fisherman has three ages: when he wants to catch as many fish as he can, when he wants to catch big fish, and when he strives to catch the most difficult fish. This works, as far as it goes. I gave four years to one stream that guarded its best fish as bees guard their queens. The Meath Blackwater flowed through farmyards, but the trout were the wildest ever, made so by pike and otters and centuries of Irishmen fishing *worrrums*. The big fish were selective. To fool them, we got up early in the mornings and sat down to our vises, calling on the genies in pots of strong tea to tie better caddisflies, and that was the fun of it. (Some fish are difficult because they are stupid. Brown trout are difficult because they are not as stupid as anglers. It is a good difficulty because it has causes, effects, and solutions, when we are clever enough to find them.)

If I could choose a week now on any stream, the Meath Blackwater would still be the one, which would make it best of all except that it's gone. We killed it: not we anglers, but we humans. I watched its death throes, and they stirred a kind of desperate love. So Hewitt did not identify the final stage of a fisherman, after all.

The best stream still living is the one that has survived the most humans. Transmigrated anglers, however, are not as easy to measure as biomass; their quantification awaits a more sensitive spectrometer. Meanwhile you can hear them whispering on the Itchen if you study to be quiet. A last snipe winnows, the sky fades behind red clouds, and there is an evening rise of several things, including Izaak Walton from Winchester Cathedral. You might interest him in a Dun Fly: Its age was already measured in centuries when he wrote about it in 1653. The trout, however, incline toward Skues's Sherry Spinner, which is old enough for me. We Yanks know how to welcome ghosts when we get the chance.

Another kind of thirst comes from a steep hike and is slaked by water innocent of history. The canyon is old as the mountains, as young as Eden. Crowds do not muddy the currents because there is little for them above the falls. What I remember best between trips is the way riffles spill into pools. An ice-age boulder may be responsible for backing up the water, but a log peeled in the spring runoff can do it too, and sometimes the stream just runs out of breath. Reflections from little waves fade into darkness and depth. Limbs overhang the outside of the pool's curve.

When some of my friends were being held hostage in a place far from home, I resolved that if I were ever in their place I would cling to these images. I would paint them on the bounds of my spirit in the way some people paper office walls with outdoor scenes.

For nonfishermen, such pictures are pretty in a general way, but flat. An angler sees another dimension under that imaginary X on the water—the secret place I try to show to my son. It is as good to see as a soul, and as elusive. Look close: Rays from a distant lens bounce off cliffs, filter through leaves, and focus dimly on a wild trout. It is surrounded by concentric rings. Of these, the first is speckled skin; the last is sky; in between are mountains and songs of veeries and cool running water.

This stream is best.

Limestone

This is about the spring creeks that bubble up from the limestone of Pennsylvania's Cumberland Valley. I want you to see them and love them and know their trout. I want you to see the limestone country, too, and know a little of its history, because there are things worth knowing. I won't give you a fly shop's guide, a real-estate pamphlet, or a hero-angler's tale. I'll give you a lover's tale—romance without cosmetics. Sometimes the lover is frustrated.

THE LIMESTONE COUNTRY

As to the Cumberland Valley, you should know that it is not a valley, has no Cumberland River, and does not even lie entirely within the modern boundaries of Cumberland

County. If you are a map person, this may spare you some puzzlement.

If there were a map for anglers, however, this area would be called the limestone country. Its flat, low-lying parts have fertile streams and fertile soil (for farmers who don't mind plowing rocks). The steep part is covered by second-growth forest, and from the hills flow small streams—not spring creeks—that may have been good for trout when the environment was primitive but are marginal now.

The waters of the non-Cumberland non-Valley run in all directions. Most of them end, after a great deal of winding and merging, in the Susquehanna River. Falling Springs Creek flows to the Potomac. Salt water is never far away, but there is a thermal barrier between trout and Atlantic: warm water where bass and catfish and sunfish can survive, but not salmonids. More accurately, there are spring-fed headwaters where isolated pockets of trout survive. Their scarcity makes them doubly prized, as with all jewels.

Americans have been angling for the limestone-country trout since frontier days. Carlisle was on the edge of civilization then, and the army built a base which is today the Army War College. (I have given seminars in its old red-brick buildings and then sneaked out to fish the lower Letort River where it winds through the campus. Caught some trout, too.)

The region has other old buildings of red brick and white frame, some of them with log-cabin skeletons underneath. Best of all are the farmhouses of gray limestone. These, at least, are so obviously beautiful that they are often restored. Many of the frame and brick houses have been torn down, rented out, or just abandoned, like old churches on the main streets of small towns. Some of the local folks have moved to new houses—the kind with shiny siding. It's not that they think it looks better. They want what is underneath the siding: insulation. Old houses don't have that, and Americans today like to live at a steady, draft-free temperature.

The limestone country is at the south end of the North, butted right up against the Mason-Dixon line. Occasional winters are northern enough to push pheasants into a farmer's barn and then freeze them. Summers are southern enough to push trout to the headwaters and then simmer them. It is a region of humid air and dry streams, like most of eastern America.

I love it just the same—because it gave me blessed relief from Washington, D.C., in the years I lived there. This is a personal history (like most histories), and for me the best things about Washington were the roads leading away from it. If this were even a half-century earlier, I would have thought the limestone country the best place in all of America. It is still one of the best on the East Coast—and this is the biggest of its problems. There are pretty small towns within easy range of the cities, and the climate is not as sultry as in some of the other places where our forefathers did their forefathering. And so the population has more than doubled since I started fishing the limestone country. Cars creep through old Chambersburg. Chic shoppes blossom on the banks of the Letort. Once when I took my family on a weekend fishing trip, we got stuck in a miles-long jam of cars heading for a car-parts fair.

The spring creeks are at the bottom of the heap—literally. They run not on the forested hillsides but in the lowest valleys, where people live, sewage drains, and interstate highways follow the path of least resistance. On some of the

Letort, the banks shake from trucks blasting by, and there are not many stretches that can still be called beautiful. The pattern of small riparian holdings has been hard on the fishing, too; few landowners have had economic incentives to restore their streams. Even so, the news is not all bad. Some of the people who loved the limestone streams to death are now trying to love them back to life.

CRADLE OF AMERICAN FLY FISHING?

Well, no. American fly fishing did not start in America. It had its origins in Britain and Ireland—misty islands some distance east of Pennsylvania. But there was, if not a cradle, at least a sort of American barbell of angling, with a bulge in the Catskills down through the Poconos and another bulge in the limestone country of south central Pennsylvania. There are good limestone streams elsewhere in Pennsylvania—Penn's Creek and Spruce Creek in the middle of the state, for example—but that was Indian country back when Carlisle needed an army base.

The writers who fished in the barbell left their mark. Theodore Gordon, for example, ended in the Catskills but began (or at least fished from the age of fourteen) in the Cumberland Valley, "where there are many fine streams that gush forth in full volume from a great spring or springs in the solid limestone rocks of that section."[1] Gordon is the first American whose accounts I can easily understand, because he fished in the ways that you and I fish today.

General George Gibson, on the other hand, was an antique, but he must have known how to handle his tackle. He began using it in 1790, in the big old Cumberland

County. There he found "three good trout streams"—Big Spring, the "Letart," and Silver Springs. The last had "the largest and best trout in the State. They are from one to three pounds...."[2] And back then all were all wild, native brook trout. Once Gibson landed twenty in a hour on flies. (The biggest wild brook trout I have caught in the limestone country was smaller than the smallest he mentioned.)

At Big Spring, Gibson also met Laughing Joe, who "makes his own lines and flies, holds a rod eighteen feet long and throws thirty-six or forty feet of line with one hand. . . ."[3] This is the kind of thing that puzzles me about so many old American accounts. I have an ancient eighteen-foot rod that is difficult to hold off the ground, let alone cast, with one hand. How did Laughing Joe do it? And did he cast his flies up- or downstream? How far did he let them sink? He must have been skilled, because the water was hard fished even then.

Theodore Gordon helps us to understand. On opening day, he says, there would be a hundred anglers on Big Spring, and the total catch would add up to three or four thousand trout. "The native anglers made their own rods of two pieces of hickory, lashed or ferruled together and painted green. Usually they cared not for a reel," and they used but one fly. Later, Gordon found the same stream ideal for dry flies.[4] And old anglers told me that Big Spring stayed good till after the Second World War, with brook trout rising for small mayflies.

The strangest thing about the history—stranger even than one-handed eighteen-foot hickory rods—is that until recently the limestone spring creeks made so little impact on American anglers and angling methods. There are repeated references like this one from 1911: "Difficulties we have to overcome, but they are not the difficulties of the English chalk stream."[5] Fishing conditions are in fact much the same on British chalk streams and American limestoners. Theodore Gordon did not understand that, but he had never been to England. Edward R. Hewitt did not understand either, and he *had* been to England.

Vincent Marinaro understood. He must have made the connection between limestone and chalk by reading, because he did not actually visit the chalk streams till long after he published *A Modern Dry-Fly Code* in 1950. There had been other good American writers, but none had grasped British precedents well enough to build on them. It was not till 1950 that we got our first angling work that did not have to start by reinventing the wheel. The book sprang from the streams of the limestone country.

STENOTHERMAL WATERS

Limestone spring creeks and chalk streams are not the same but they are chemically similar, and the chemistry provides high fertility. Equally important, they are stenothermal—meaning that their temperatures fluctuate in a narrow range, relative to that of streams fed directly by rain or snowmelt. (In Pennsylvania, these latter streams are called "freestone"—as opposed to limestone—waters. My dictionary does not give a definition for "freestone" in this sense, and in most of the world the term is not used.)

Streams that issue from springs should not form anchor ice in the winter or reach temperatures lethal to trout in the summer. Further, water volumes are *relatively* constant when streams elsewhere are in drought or flood. I have, nevertheless, seen both the Letort and Falling Springs Creek when local downpours made them too high and dirty to fish. The Yellow Breeches has important rainwater sources.

There are spring creeks in the west that are today in better condition than the Pennsylvania limestoners. There are tailwater fisheries that provide the same kind of fishing, and more of it, without sources in springs. Our fly-fishing boom of recent years has focused on these rich streams. We have by no means stopped fishing in the less-fertile waters, but our books and our fishing schools have emphasized the techniques of stenothermal streams. Such waters can produce heavy hatches and rising fish, which we catch, or try to catch, with imitative flies—those that match the hatch. The fish often feed visibly on or near the surface, so we use many dry flies or near-surface nymphs. It is a kind of hunting, really: stalking and aiming at a visible quarry rather than waiting for something mysterious to happen in the depths. The people who are drawn to fly fishing in the first place often seem especially drawn to this particular kind.

THE SPRING CREEKS TODAY

The Pennsylvania limestone streams, then, offer a sport of special attractions to the residents of Megalopolis. In the absence of private waters, the offer is almost without costs and restrictions. And so, of course, the fishing has drawn crowds that seem enormous by comparison to those of the 1960s. I have stayed as far as possible from the crowds. This is why my personal limestone map is different from most.

You have to decide, first, whether to fish on your schedule or nature's. Perhaps the best time for you is a Sunday afternoon. You drive to the Letort Spring Run after a late breakfast, park, and wander where the mood takes you. It feels good. You don't catch much, but you were not expecting to do so; everybody has told you what a difficult stream this is.

If you want to fish during convenient hours, there is an alternative: Go where there is a concentration of trout willing to take a deep nymph at any time. You could try the Yellow Breeches. It had a put-and-grow stocking program when I was last there, and the fish wised up after they had been caught a few times—which usually did not take long. There was a concentration of anglers, too.

Alternatively, you could time your visits to hit the hatches, but nature's schedule is not convenient. Tricos provide the most abundant and long-lasting of hatches, but it comes in the early morning, or even late at night if the weather is unusually hot.

The Letort has had its troubles—the usual assortment, plus insecticides that washed down from the cress beds at the headwaters—but of all the limestoners, it is the only one that improved while I was watching. Earlier in this century, sewage from the town of Carlisle had turned the lower part of the Letort from a brook-trout stream into a sewer. A new sewage-treatment facility changed that.

Vince Marinaro is often associated with the upper Letort in writing, so I should mention that he liked the lower part better. He showed it to me at sunrise on July 20, 1985, right after I had returned from a tour of duty in Europe. Vince's bad hip made walking difficult by then, so he waded into the river right below a bridge and spent the whole Trico hatch casting to a few fish that he had been educating all summer.

I roamed a mile of the stream. There were a lot of rising brown trout—most of which had been stocked as finger-lings—and they took flies without caution. The fish breeders had managed to perfect a strain of browns as stupid as the usual hatchery rainbows. I worried about the impact of degenerate genes on the old Letort strain. Fortunately, most of the stocked fish could not figure out how to reproduce. (I watched them trying in the fall.)

The rise was over by midmorning, so Vince guided me to other access points just for a look. The stream had good pools and runs everywhere. Vince said that he'd been watching it through the years and thinking how wonderful it could be. Now that it had trout instead of sewage, he was delighted.

Big Spring Creek, near Newville, is of all the limestone-country streams the one I would have been most eager to fish fifty years ago. Before I got to it, however, water quality col-lapsed, and with it the populations of brook trout and mayflies. The stream was taken over by cress bugs (alias sow bugs or water lice). At a Trout Unlimited meeting, we asked state fisheries biologists about this, and one of them said: "We can't manage a stream for invertebrates." It was a mem-orable position—about like a dairy farmer refusing to con-sider the condition of his pasture. Perhaps attitudes have changed. This stream has a single source in a spring that is indeed big, so it could be cleaned up more easily than most. It always did have some good brown trout in its lower reach-es for diligent seekers of truth.

Falling Springs Creek, near Chambersburg, is so small in the midst of its meadows that insects are bound to fall in, so an occasional trout can be found rising to terrestrials even dur-ing the off-hours. And when I fished there, water quality was the way Tricos liked it: not bad but not pristine, either. Most anglers had not yet figured out how to fish the Trico hatch, and I had stretches to myself on summer dawns. But the stream's wild rainbows—unusual in this part of the country—were almost gone. Some of the stream was barren of fish, but other sections had wild browns, a few of which got big by eating other trout. Some dedicated people were working hard to restore the stream with a Falling Springs greenway.

Over the years, I sampled all of the well-known limestone streams and others not so well known. Silver Springs and Green Spring Creek had some fishing but were not as good as the Letort. There were other little spring creeks too. Some of them are still there, but I heard of one that was paved over for an interstate highway.

Spring-fed streams—those that are left—can be maintained or reclaimed if enough of us want badly enough to do it. I've watched the process in England and participated in it in Montana. (In both cases, admittedly, the pattern of land ownership provides more incentives.) You cut off sources of pollution and fence the banks to prevent trampling by cattle. You put in stream improvements to restore pools and clean gravel for spawning. You shore up crumbling banks. If you can afford it, you get into the stream with heavy equipment that lifts out silt and corrects decades of abuse in a few days. It looks like a violent cure but it works splendidly when it's done right.

What do we do with the reclaimed streams? We go fishing in them. There are a lot of us, and God isn't making trout streams anymore. We have seldom been successful in apportioning access to public streams. Americans chafe under such restrictions.

Can we learn to manage success?

NOTES

(1) Theodore Gordon, *The Complete Fly Fisherman,* ed. John McDonald (New York: The Lyons Press, 1989), 111.

(2) Austin S. Hogan, "Bob Fly, Dropper-Tail Fly, Stretcher" *The American Fly Fisher* 3, no. 4 (Fall 1976): 12.

(3) Ibid.

(4) Gordon, *The Complete Fly Fisherman,* 112, 188.

(5) E. B. Rice, "Where to Use the Dry Fly." In Leonard M. Wright Jr., ed., *"The Field Stream Treasury of Trout Fishing* (New York: The Lyons Press, 1986), 31.

A Place of Our Own

My wife wanted a nest; I wanted total immersion in nature; and both of us wanted a home, after moving from one crowded city to another all those years. We built between spring creek and pond, and by now all of us have weathered: boards, dogs, and people. Anna calls our Montana home a house, but I think of it as a permanent blind, gray and low. In shape it is octagonal, which is as circular as we could make it (bearing in mind that nature is round). Wide porches taper the walls into fields, and there are big windows on every side except the cold north.

We've been here fifteen years now, but an owl perched on the chimney keeps asking, "Who, who who, who, whooo?"—as if he didn't know us by now. Anna is the small person filling the bird-feeder, and I am the face at the window, glancing back and forth between my work and my world.

Some great horned owls catch fish, and our chimney would be a good perch for spotting them. This bird, however, never lets us know what he has in mind. He is a philosopher by day and by night a predator, feeding on things that quiver in the dark. Come dawn, my dog shows me the piles of duck or pheasant feathers, but a trout's death seldom leaves clues.

Getting Particular

Wildlife of one kind or another uses all of the land and water, fanning out from a marshy core that has survived without much change—over the years since Lewis and Clark passed through—simply because it is too wet to plow and too brushy for cattle. You can sit in the shade of a cottonwood and watch whatever show is playing. Yesterday the actors were snipe drumming, baby teal skittering after midges, sandhill cranes dancing, and sora rails practicing their ventriloquist act.

This is not paradise, mind you—not when you learn the problems—and sixty acres are hardly enough to give two people and three pointing dogs everything we need in life. None of us are complaining, though. We've done time on pavement, and this is better.

When you add water to a piece of Montana, you bring to the surface a curious, postglacial fertility. Painted turtles crawl from the pond for what must be their mating season (though it's hard to be sure, with a turtle) and diving ducks drop in on their way to Canada. Just once a loon called while we were having breakfast and got me so stirred up that I spilled tea on my jeans.

SPRING CREEK

The problem with still water, in this climate, is that ice keeps some birds and mammals away for three or four months. Meanwhile the spring creek remains open, a winding corridor with riffles and pools and deep dark holes where monsters could hide.

Here in the family, we began calling it Humility Creek—not so much a philosophical statement as a reflection on the eyes of fly fishers slinking homeward. The brown trout at least had the courtesy to feed discreetly, but the rainbows got you talking to yourself. They would lie in midstream, taking every mayfly that came by, except for the one with a hook in it.

Research was in order. I began marking each trout I could land by clipping its adipose fin, then releasing it and trying to catch it again. What I found was embarrassing: These fish learn faster than us humans. Few trout in Humility Creek fall for a fly twice in the same year.

Somewhere along the banks, however, there is a better fisherman. The heron moves in geologic time. I cannot keep up with its slowness. But when I look again, the great gangly bird has a squirming rainbow in its beak.

Heron works the day shift, taking fish all year and ducklings in season. Sometimes I spook the big bird from sedges where baby mallards hide, but it sneaks back, skinny as Don Quixote and far more deadly with a spear. In winter, when the weeds die back, the great blue heron spears even spawning fish that are too big to swallow, and by spring, most surviving trout carry the triangular brand of the heron's lower beak. A rainbow last May had four spear marks. Other trout run downstream to bigger water for the winter months, and I suspect that the heron has something to do with this migratory pattern.

One heron broke its wing, perhaps on a power line, and I managed to stop my dog as he was moving in to investigate. A warden then came out and shot the bird before anyone got hurt. I have read, but cannot confirm, the story of a woman who was speared in the throat and killed by a heron she was trying to rescue.

Heron is the teacher. He does not fish on general principles and neither do you, his student—not unless you want a humility lesson. You sneak up on one particular trout till you can see its spots. You figure out that it is taking duns in the surface film, and then you offer the fly it expects to see. You watch first and cast later.

And the same is true for other problems on the place. You don't just do something. You stand there. But you keep your eyes open, like the great blue heron.

The osprey's method is the opposite of the heron's—surprise, not stealth. The osprey is too big to hover gracefully, but its aim is accurate and it plunges at a speed that seems life-threatening to both fish and fish-hawk. A moment after the splash, the bird emerges and flounders off with a midsized trout flopping in locked claws. The victim is likely to be a bold rainbow that was too far from cover, rising for mayflies.

After all that work, the osprey may lose its catch to the bald eagle, which Benjamin Franklin called "a bird of bad moral character . . . too lazy to fish for himself." I watch eagles flying over the creek looking for prey, but I seldom see them eating anything except previously owned trout and ground squirrels, alias gophers, which are pushovers when they're young. Last spring four eagles plundered the osprey, gormandized the gophers, and perched in the cottonwood trees to recover. I cannot swear that I heard the sound of burping.

Give me plenty of bald eagles, all the same. They are beautiful and they must be tough, because the owl lies low when they are around and the heron is inclined to fish elsewhere.

Wonder if I could get an eagle interested in pelicans? They are pure spectacle, massive white triangles soaring out of the Cretaceous. There is no other species that I would rather watch—at high altitude. Fortunately, they make several passes before splashdown, giving me time to bound out the door. Usually they decide that this creek is not big enough for all of us. Clumsy as they look, they know how to herd and scoop trout, and that pouch would hold a lot of them.

The pelicans head south for the winter, thank goodness, but the spring creek stays open for business and a kingfisher hangs around. It is built for survival on short rations, small and perky. Well, sort of perky. My personal kingfisher does not sit on the end of a limb and brag, like kingfishers in more peaceful country. I think he's worried about the bigger birds hooting and diving and plundering around this place.

LEARNING TO SEE

In principle, I don't like lawns, which goes to show that you can't manage land on general principles. Take my lazy-man's yard, for example. After an adjoining field burned, I developed a keen interest in the firebreak around our house, and from there one thing led to another. White-tailed deer—supposedly browsers—spent winter nights cropping the grass. In return they left genuine organic fertilizer pellets, which revived growth early in spring. And that ring of green grass turned into a circus.

The opening act was a snipe (presumably female) who trundled over the short grass, pursued by others (presumably male) who were acting like jerks. She pretended to ignore them. At about the same time, several killdeers appointed themselves night watchmen, and a pair of spotted sandpipers hatched young so tiny that they could barely navigate the dandelions. A harrier took an interest in the chicks but I shooed him off.

Conclusion: One lawn per sixty acres creates an edge effect, attracting wildlife. It is not a problem and does not need fixing.

But you seldom get so lucky. A farm is, by definition, an ecology altered to feed humans, and you have to remember where you fit in the food chain. You don't take possession, exactly, but you take responsibility.

There are stories—some accurate—about folks who love the pretty purple flowers on their construction site. And no wonder. Knapweed is the most carefree ground cover there is, short of the plastic turf in stadiums. With knapweed, you needn't worry about harriers eating sandpipers. You won't have any sandpipers. You won't have much wildlife of any kind.

My backpack sprayer controls knapweed and other noxious Eurasian plants, but it is a sweaty, smelly, never-ending job. The trick is to work up a warlike mood. Our teenager would be good at spot-spraying if he weren't busy at his computer,

game. Today, the large predators are in this valley are us—the humans—and we come equipped with wide-angle lenses. We see woods and fields as islands of tranquility in an ugly urban world. When I zoom in, however, nature is not peaceful and certainly not stable. The white-tailed deer, for example, have outgrown their food supply.

Late on a November afternoon, there comes an opportunity to prune the herd selectively. Deer feed in an open field, and I sneak to its edge through brush, reversing the normal habitat of hunter and whitetail. There is time to pick a doe—preferably one who lost this year's twins but will breed again soon. A bipod keeps the crosshairs steady on her heart. I don't want to do this, for some quaint masculine reason, but she is plump and she will taste better than one of us raunchy old bucks.

Give me a C for management of deer. They are still browsing back any brush without thorns, but at least the herd has not built up to a bust.

With ducks, make the grade a D. When I looked up from work just now, the creek was full of green heads, yellow beaks, and wiggles—mallard drakes in courtship display. Another drake has just dropped in, wings cupped, orange feet down as if landing in decoys. What concerns me (and the bachelor drakes) is that only one hen has shown up for the party.

I think I know why the hens are scarce. My steady old dog helps me with an annual informal census, and finding nests is a cinch for him. It may be equally easy for the skunks—who won't stop on point.

Some good-sized broods nevertheless hatch and reach the stream, where I see Ms. Mallard with eleven fuzzy ducklings the first day, then nine, six, five, three.

The problem is habitat, and no matter what we do, this habitat favors small predators over prey. The valley has ever more people and uncontrolled pets. More houses produce more roving cats, more gigantic tame geese, more fragmented cover for the magpies, and more trees for the great horned owls. It all looks nice, though—unless you're a duck.

Biologists' studies confirm that ducks are having trouble staying ahead of predators and competitors. Trappers can help to even the balance, but low fur prices provide little incentive.

COSTS AND BENEFITS

I am aiming for the ecology of an old-fashioned farm with small fields, hedgerows, marshes, and trees—not the best of all possible worlds, but the best available.

The hay field is in a mixture of alfalfa and grass, which is good cover for nesting pheasants but must not be cut before they are off the nest. The other field is in barley, which the deer will eat if it is left standing too long. When harvested, however, some grain spills on the ground for ducks, pheasants, cranes, and passerine birds.

There are costs. Alfalfa harvested late can lose value, and a field of barley left in stubble is harder to work when spring comes around. You give up a little of the income from other crops to produce wildlife. In economic terms, game is a crop, too.

When you fish or hunt, on the other hand, your game becomes "God's meat" (Aldo Leopold's term). The investment is economic; the returns come in a different currency.

Psychic rewards are hard to measure, but perhaps the marketplace shows a way. Diversity outsells monoculture. Land with both wildlife and crops goes for a higher price than "clean" fields. The difference, I suppose, shows how much people like to live with wild things.

Liberation

The Mondego River plunges from Portugal's highest range, cuts through the steepest gorge, and dawdles past the oldest university. The flow sections the nation's land and people: granite and shepherds at the top, then terraces and peasants, bottomlands and farmers, streets and students, salt marshes and shipyards.

Adriano and I drove from ocean to headwaters in one afternoon, climbing through all the strata, determined to drink from the Mondego's source and cower in its canyon. Next day at dawn we looked down at the river—half blue, half foamy white, and small at the bottom of its canyon. Adriano showed me the goat trail down through the rocks.

I rushed to assemble my rod and tie on a team of three Portuguese wet flies. They should have been good before the sun warmed the water. I cast upstream through the pools, letting the flies drift back past me, deep. Then I fished cross-stream and watched the line swing around in the current. When all else failed, I teased the top fly along the surface, the two below it serving to keep my leader straight. It is a good method for eager trout, but these weren't.

We came to an eddy that had created a little foothold for alders. A bird was dancing in them, but I paid attention only to my flies swinging under the brush, troutless. The bird still danced. It was a desperate dance, but then I was getting desperate myself. The flutter came again and I saw that the victim was a *pintasilgo* (English goldfinch) of sweet song. I waded the stream, boots shipping water. The finch had tried to eat a trout fly that someone had cast across the stream with a spinning rod. The float had caught in the alders, the line had broken, and the fly had dangled, a cruel trap. I unhooked the bird and held it for a moment to calm down, soft black and yellow body quiet in my caress, scarlet face looking at me. When I opened my hand the finch lay for a moment, not realizing that it was free, and then flashed off through green leaves.

My own line had been dangling in the current below me during the rescue operation. I waded back to shore, cleaned the flies of some flotsam they had picked up, and cast them to the upstream end of the eddy. My intention was just to get the line straightened out so that I could wind it back evenly onto the reel. Chances of catching anything after that commotion were slim. But the line twitched as it drifted under a limb and I pulled the rod tight. A strong trout flashed gold, hooked on the top fly. I trotted her downstream at once, keeping the angle between me and fish constant till she tired and slid into my net. She was a brown trout, Portuguese native of antecedents older than Adriano's. As I released her, my back began to feel warm and little glints reflected from the current. The sun was up.

There is a modest claim that I may make: I have liberated myself from trophies and scores. It was not difficult—not like liberation from fear, which only a few heroes achieve. Mostly I just got older. Once I had dreamt of catching big trout, read books about how to do it, and chased them from Patagonia to Donegal. When I catch one now, I am still pleased. It is a gift, but it is not a triumph.

The scores were a phase, too. I learned to return most of my trout to the water, unharmed, and thought that numbers were needed to document my prowess. It was nonconsumptive consumerism, a competition without messy dead fish.

Now that my affair with trout has progressed through sophistication to the primitive, I am free to pursue a two-little-fish dinner in bliss. There is comfort in the relationship enjoyed by the first people who hunted food in these streams after the glacier. The method is different and the restraints are stronger—must be, in these days of fewer trout and more anglers—but the emotion is the same. I feel sure of this. Fishing is a kind of archaeology, a way of excavating layers, digging into strata built by my ancestors, finding an underground river.

Adriano stopped casting and started looking for a trail up the hill. I fished with redoubled ferocity. He told me that he knew of a field of wild strawberries and would have a look for it on the way back to the village. I was to feel free to fish as long as I wished. I did wish, for some reason of incomprehensible hunger, but pretended that I did not and tagged along.

The strawberries were almost as scarce as the trout. We had to get on our knees and search through the grass for red beads. They were good but they did not flee, so I lost interest. (Adolescent males, including overgrown ones like me, are all hunters. Older men are content to be gatherers. Gathering may require a higher level of consciousness, if by "higher" you mean older and therefore closer to heaven. Then again, some of the things we call levels of consciousness may be layers of platitudes.)

We worked our way up the hill in stages. A little boy somewhere was calling for a strayed kid, urging it back to the fold before night came, and the wolves. Closer to us, a blackbird sang to the setting sun from a thicket of pines. There was no hint in his song of complaint or aggression. The melody rippled out like goats' bells across the valley, or like the bright stream over its boulders. I did not care what the ornithologists might think: That blackbird was singing the song I hum when I fish for little wild trout.

PART THREE

The Way of a Fly with a Trout

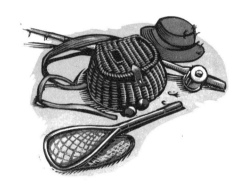

The Winged Life

*S*pring comes in a sunburst of life. Caddisfly pupae feel the warmth, leave their nutritious soup at the bottom of the stream, and climb toward a rim of light. You cast to the first splashy rise. A winter-thin brown trout takes your fly and, by the time it is dry and ready for bigger fish, grannoms are landing on your ears, laying egg sacs on your waders, and everywhere hopping, skittering, and shattering the mirror of water. With so much competition from nature, you may not catch much. But you feel the surge of energy, and you too will crawl from your winter husk.

In Pursuit of Trout and Virtue

*. . . doubt not but Angling will prove to be so pleas-
ant, that it will prove itself to be like virtue, a reward
to itself. . . .*

—Izaak Walton

In March the sap began to rise in this valley's willows and anglers. The trees expressed themselves in little furry catkins and, I suppose, some contributions of pollen, while the fly fishers announced that they would offer an exposition. Naturally I went along to see what was being exposed.

In the gym, athletes of both sexes—but mostly young— were working miracles with long fly rods. Pink and orange and (I think) fuchsia lines flickered under the ceiling, reaching nearly to one wall on the backcast and the opposite end on the shoot. If you wanted to fly fish at what used to be surf-casting distances, this was the place to learn. And besides, you had to admire any instructor who could get a suntan like that before the daffodils bloomed.

The other big room was lined with benches for fly tying, which hurts less than casting for those of us who have donated our elbows to the cause, and the expositors were inclined to a touch of gray at the temples. These folks were not recent converts to fly fishing. On the contrary, they had come to help the scores of new anglers attracted by a booming sport.

Fly fishing used to be a quiet thing for the few of us who lived in the right places, read the right magazines, or otherwise received the vision. By the 1950s, some of us were trying to get other people involved—especially people of the female persuasion—but the ones I interviewed did not care for swatting and there wasn't a good mosquito repellent on the market.

Most of us tied our own flies then, if only because it was hard to find good representations of American trout-stream insects. Until 1969, no one I knew could have identified the little mayflies that produced our most abundant hatches. And very few would have ventured a size-22 Trico imitation like the one Charlie Loveless was tying at the exposition.

Charlie told me that he had decided to tie his own flies because he could not find the ones he needed on the market. What began as necessity, however, "evolved into therapy." He had high-pressure work in Washington, D.C., and tying helped to "erase the tape." You would recognize Charlie's old job, but I won't mention it because he did not describe himself as an ex-anything, and neither did the four other people I talked to. These active-duty anglers are at their peak right now.

For Dave Knickerbocker, it all began with a fly-tying kit. His first flies were rough, but he took them on a trip to Colorado just the same and found a way to cast them on a bait-casting rod. Flies are what trout eat, as he points out, and he caught four rainbows despite his crude tackle. It was "the most excitement I'd ever had in my life," he said. He was shy about root causes, like most of us, but I sat looking at the flies he ties today, which are anything but crude, and he added that fly fishing is "trying to find your soul."

Of all the stories at that exposition, only Syl Nemes's began in Cleveland. No tackle shop in Ohio would have featured Catskill dry flies—not so far from their locus—but a barber displayed them in his window and Syl admired them and taught himself to tie his own flies two years before he met the kind of fish who would reward work like that.

I noticed that trout flies had hooked Syl Nemes and Dave Knickerbocker before either of them hooked his first trout. The sequence was the same for me, if you don't mind me interviewing myself. I was eleven years old when I saw an artificial fly in *Life* magazine and copied it, more or less, with yarn from Mom and a plume from my pillow. When I wound the feather on a hook, its fibers sprang into a cavalier's ruff and I was passing proud to have reinvented the hackle. It must have been a beautiful fish, I thought, to have caused such a thing to be created.

For Rocky Miller, it was not the fly but the fishing that caught the man. "Falling in love with the rhythm," he called it, and hunting had the same feeling. I should explain here that Rocky makes longbows that bend and sing like fly rods.

"It's the way you look at life," he said. "You can take it to any level."

Ken Ligas fished for the right words, starting in shallow water. "It's just so much fun to catch a trout on a fly you've tied yourself," he said. "Once you do that, you're hooked for life."

I sat there listening (which gets easier with practice) and Ken waded deeper. Fishing is a kind of freedom, he said, and it comes with "using the creativity each of us has hidden inside. . . . You come up with an idea and assemble it with bits of fur and feather and tinsel. You bring it to life. It's as close as you ever get to being God."

Who Needs That Dumb Fish?

Angling is a game you can't lose, if that's any consolation. Here you are, one human surrounded by a dozen rising trout and ten thousand insects having the best day of their lives. True, you have only one fly on your leader, which means that the odds are against you, but even if the trout ignore your offer ninety-nine times in a row, you can always try again. You might even catch a fish eventually, and the fish will never catch you.

Suppose that you have waded into the best position you can reach near a rising trout, made your best cast—and watched the fish reject your fly. There is a good chance that some vagary of the current made the fly drag. Perhaps you could not see its slight unnatural movement, but the trout could. The next step, in this case, is not just to change from a little gray dry fly to a little tan dry fly. Instead, pick a new design, one that fishes at a different level. Try an extra-high-floating dry fly or a near-surface nymph, for example. Either of them might let you get away with a little drag.

This is supposed to be fun, so experiment first with the high-floating design—one that drifts with the whole hook out of the water, point and all. The flies called variants, spiders, and skaters all float high because they use big hackles. Better still, try the fore-and-aft design, which has a tightly wound hackle at each end—small in the front and just long-fibered enough in the rear to cover the point of the hook. Trout take this fly with more confidence than the big, bushy kind.

The advantage of any high-floating design is mobility. When it threatens to drag, you can give it a twitch, let it resume a natural float, and twitch it again. You can even dance it over the water like a cranefly in mating ecstasy. Trout may wake up and pounce. Unfortunately, they may also slash at the fly, miss it, and then repent their reckless behavior. Fish are not very adventurous, when you get down to it, and they don't want us to enjoy ourselves either.

All right, then. Try a near-surface nymph. Some of the events that look like rises are really the tips of tails coming out of the water—which means that the trout is taking sub-surface food. It also means that you cannot not tell one end of a fish from the other.

And when you figure it out, this is finicky fishing. You cannot get away with strike indicators, split shot, big hooks wrapped with lead wire, or any of that heavy-metal stuff. Instead, try a fine tippet three feet long. At the end, tie on an unweighted nymph in size 16, 18, or 20. A slim body of pheasant-tail herl or hare's ear often works, and you want just a wisp of hackle or a few fibers of hair at the front to keep the fly from sinking too fast. Grease the tippet with fly flotant down to within a few inches of the end, but then soak the nymph in your mouth. (What's good enough for a trout is good enough for you.) Get the fly in the water a yard upstream from the rising fish, and watch as if you had a Scots accent—*verrry* carefully.

If the trout moves at all, or opens its mouth, tighten your line quickly and gently, because a violent strike will pop the leader. Do it right and you get to chase up and down the stream for five minutes after a fish that is trying to break your three-hundred-dollar rod. All of us anglers agree that this is fun.

If you should then eat the trout, which is good for your health, remember to check its stomach contents first. Not always, but usually, you will find that a fish feeding on the surface was also taking natural nymphs that happened to drift by a couple of inches deeper. And because those insects were floundering, the trout was willing to accept an imitation that may have been dragging slightly—because of an involuntary twitch in your elbow.

Fly on Dark Water

There is a time machine in running water. You wade in and watch the toes of your boots settling down, welcoming little eddies of sand. The stream pulses clear but has enough texture to wash you. Aspen leaves drift down the current and your heart slows to match their diaspora. They linger because they will not make this trip again, and the home they are losing is the one you have gained.

When you reach the shade, you leave the weight of a century spinning down toward town with the leaves. The current now is dark and broken and a hundred years deep with things you want to discover, so you tie on a Royal Coachman to guide you.

Perhaps you choose this old pattern because you want the twentieth century to stay lost. Magic is part of fishing, and the Royal Coachman has more experience as a totem than any other American fly. But perhaps, instead, you want something that you can see in deep shade, and after all these years a Coachman, Royal or plain, is still hard to beat on your dark little stream. I may finally have understood why.

There has been an eclosion of knowledge about the things trout eat, and new information has changed the flies fishermen carry. Some fly shops do not even sell wet flies anymore. Of the modern dry flies and nymphs, many are better than the old products of folklore, but the new ones do tend to be imitative—of aquatic insects and of each other.

Hatch matching, in short, is no longer a lonely sport. As a teenager, I could hitchhike to the Firehole River, try to catch its rising trout, then peel off and float down through braids of warm-spring water, bothering no one. Today a gross of brother anglers would curse my imitation of a white whale, and three of their spouses would start writing novels. The entire California population, plus half that of the East Coast, now makes a summer migration to the spring creeks and fertile rivers of the Rocky Mountains. These folks carry flies with Latin names.

But there are other streams with few hatches. All over our land there are creeks small and shaded, because trees and cliffs have a way of growing near water. There are granite boulders, light and shadow, broken currents. For generations of fishermen these small streams have been an escape, a joy, a dark passion. They are as pretty as the wild trout in them. The fish, however, seldom reveal their presence by rising. You must search the water, casting where a trout might be, believing that it is there, never losing sight of your fly.

For this you need a fly with traditional values: not the moral kind but color values in sharp contrast, dark body and white wing. You can follow such a fly in brightest glare or darkest shade, especially if the wings are of real calf-tail hairs—shiny, irregular, and crinkly.

Under these conditions, flies that imitate aquatic insects have a fundamental defect: They are camouflaged. Think about it. Small water creatures evolved under pressure from predators like trout and swallows, finding ways to be inconspicuous. One of our masters wrote of a "hidden hatch." When your artificial fly is hidden, you cannot fish well on dappled water.

Perhaps that does not matter. If you are a poet, you fish the little rocky waters because you want their songs, and you do not mind if you catch few trout. If you are of scientific bent, you fish rivers and spring creeks with important hatches to imitate. There it is easier to learn what you are doing, as a scientist must.

In the American way, I want it all. I want the hidden streams because they do something for me that no other place does. I want to see their shiny little trout in my net, and sometimes I want to take one meal's worth home to my family to make up for the things I should have done instead of going fishing. But I want to fish not by folklore but like a scientist, knowing what I am doing and why. And I don't want a spring-creek fly for this shaded water any more than I want an out-of-sight pointer for a grouse covert.

The path up that dark stream has been a long one with few guides. The first was Edward R. Hewitt, who wrote that the fly should be "bivisible"—easily seen by both trout and fishermen. He knew that the trout saw dark flies most easily, whereas fishermen needed a flash of white. He did not, however, understand the optics of the water's surface well enough to come up with the right design. His Bivisible was a high-floating palmer fly with red-brown hackles over most of its body and a white hackle in front. Trout often did not take this well, and it took time for me to figure out their problem.

Mine was clear right away: The Bivisible was not, in fact, easy to see on dark water. Its hackle fibers were thin, flexible, and translucent—good for camouflage, not visibility. Hewitt's fly was a fair imitation of one aquatic insect (the skittering caddisfly), but it was not "bivisible" because it was neither dense nor low floating enough to take advantage of the surface optics.

Ray Bergman, angling editor of *Outdoor Life*, preferred a Fan-Wing Royal Coachman, which would flutter to the water and sit there flamboyant, for the nonce. Fish liked this better than the Bivisible, and that was the problem: A trout would soon drool on the wings, which would then shrivel into a sort of propeller, making a kamikaze sound as I cast.

A. J. McClane, fishing editor of *Field & Stream*, wrote about the Quack Coachman, which was first tied by Reuben Cross in 1930. Its hair wing was called "impala" then, but all of the impala I bought turned out to be white calf tail. It was, and is, nature's best material for the purpose—finer, lighter, and more flexible than deer hair; brighter and more dense than feathers; and shiny till the end, unlike any synthetic I have tried. The best calf-tail hairs have tiny kinks that reflect the light like a diamond's facets. And, unlike fan wings, calf-tail hair does not form an airfoil to twist the leader.

Life moved me and the Royal Coachman around, and in the Catskill streams we met classic eastern hatches. Art Flick would have been the right teacher if I'd heard of him, but I hadn't, so the old fly had to guide me on its own. It had not seen any classic bugs before and felt shy. Not to worry. "Classic," in fly-speak, turned out to mean anything written in a book twenty years earlier. The Royal Coachman was by comparison an antique, and everyone knows that antiques are classier than classics.

Thus encouraged, a sparse version of the antique caught about as many trout as anything else. No fly is always right, but white wings, at least, were visible, meaning that I hooked a larger share of the trout that rose.

Vincent Marinaro was my guide to the Pennsylvania limestone streams, and here the Royal Coachman often failed. It had the wrong shape for any aquatic insect and was too big for those hatching. But Vince knew more than anyone about the architecture of dry flies. He showed me how to make them land right side up and float well, even in the small sizes that fish love and fishermen used to hate, before his time. I learned to put Marinaro's widespread V-tail on every upwinged fly, including the Royal Coachman. That tail did by design what used to require bulk.

About this time there was another guide, of a sort: an El Dorado Parisian Brougham Imperial with three-color paint job. You could guess that it was a car because wheels were discernible, and you knew that it was from Detroit because its names were from Spain, France, Scotland, and the Austro-Hungarian Empire. This vehicle was good for my fishing because I didn't have one, and people who did stayed off dirt roads. But there was my reputation to think of. A generation of kids got seasick in the rear seat and grew up hating opera windows, and it became embarrassing to open a box of red, white, and green flies. Examined closely, the Royal Coachman even had a bulge that might have been construed as a tail fin.

One of my new flies looked like a Volkswagen, and you can guess which insect it imitated. Humans liked to talk of mayflies, but when I checked the stomachs of trout from my favorite wooded streams, there were far more beetles. And no wonder. David Quammen writes that "one of every four animals on earth (by count of the number of species) is, yes, a beetle." Now, some of the 300,000 species of beetles do not look like a ball of peacock herl, but many of those in the trout's stomachs did. You could say that the trout themselves were my guide now.

I did not choose peacock because it looked like the tail fins on a Royal Coachman. No indeed. I copied the oldest beetle fly in my books, which happened to be named a Coch-y-Bondhu, and so far nobody has put *that* on a car's side in chrome letters.

The Coch-y-Bondhu was nothing but a sparse hackle, a round beetle shape of herl, and a stout Partridge hook—wide of gape to keep the point clear of the extra-plump body. This was a dry fly except when it was wet. Other beetle flies worked on the surface but not when they sank a little—as real beetles often do. On the slow meadow streams, I could usually see the trout come to my fly, even under the surface. On fast water I couldn't.

So, of course, I put on calf-tail V-wings, short and sparse. A wisp of hair was enough to hold the Coachman suspended in the current, hovering, and perhaps tiny air bubbles caught in the crinkles reminded the fish of emerging caddisfly pupae or other insects. Marinaro's V-tail then had to be added to balance the wings and keep the fly from sinking at the rear.

Real beetles have neither tail nor visible wings: Those were for me. I needed to watch the little white V bobbing victoriously toward the maw of the trout down there. He didn't have the size of a shark, but he had the temperament and I thought of his tail beating faster as he watched my Dark-Water Fly sliding down shady currents.

So much for the magic. The science of it is that a fly can be designed for both humans and trout because we see different parts of it. You and I think of water as transparent, but its surface is, in fact, a visual barrier. A fisherman sees the part of a fly that sticks above the surface, and a trout sees best what is in or below the surface. For the fisherman, looking down, the water is typically dark, so white wings provide maximum contrast. Trout, on the contrary, look toward the light when feeding on floating insects, and seen from below, most of the surface is a silvery mirror. Maximum contrast comes from a dark, low-floating body—like peacock. Everything above the surface is indistinct or invisible, especially if pale.

Here is another way to think of it. Most fish are dark on their backs, pale on their bellies. This makes them difficult to see from both top and bottom. For a fly that is easy to see, we need a contrary design: dark below, light above. This looks wrong, but it is important. A good fishing instructor told me that the biggest problem of his students was not casting, wading, or tying knots. The hardest part was seeing the fly well enough to fish it properly.

You see now why a hair-wing Coachman, in most of its variations, remains our favorite dark-water design: With white wings and peacock body, it reverses nature's order of light and dark. I suppose nobody has explained this because we've been asking the wrong question. We've wondered for decades what insect the Royal Coachman imitates. It has succeeded because it imitates a Coupe de Ville, not a mayfly.

Reinventing the Royal Coachman is a bit like reinventing the wheel, but the fancy old fly does run into trouble, sometimes, with educated trout. The Dark-Water Fly fools more of them and is not so fussy to tie. I meant it for little freestone streams, but spring-creek trout that would not move 6 inches for a mayfly have startled me by coming across a pool for the winged beetle. They know that it is a soft target: Beetles falling in the water cannot escape and are not camouflaged like aquatic insects. One of nature's pranks was to hang on the beetle a sign that says EAT ME when he falls into the water.

I have tried changing hackle colors and adding red to the Dark-Water Fly, just to see if the fish were impressed. They were not. If there is magic in floss of red, eye of newt, or wool of bat, it is magic that impresses humans more than fish. Peacock herl, now, does seem to conjure up the trout. It has a metallic luster, and real beetles come with metallic paint jobs.

Still, every fly has to catch an angler before it catches a trout. The Royal Coachman caught your grandfather's fancy, and if it catches yours, you are welcome to it. Science and magic are both comforting on dark little streams.

A wild trout is magic enough for me. I want to see sunlight slicing a shaded pool and a jeweled fish arrowing up from the bottom for my little fly. The apparition is as quick as a camera's shutter and as slow as life. Dark water. Slanting ray of sun. Trout flashes, moment passes. Image lasts.

The Mayfly Murders

A detective story for anglers

A brown trout was waylaying insects the other morning, and a fisherman was trying to identify the victims. The scene was a fertile spring creek—the kind that often has two or more species of insects on the water at the same time. The only clue was that my imitation of a midge drifted over the trout repeatedly with no show of interest while natural flies continued to vanish in stealthy little rise-bubbles.

Fly fisherman have been investigating such cold-blooded violence since the fifteenth century, and probably longer. There are variations in the details—as you would expect from a mystery series running 500 years—but at core the plot changes little. There is a furtive wrinkle on the surface of the stream, or perhaps a violent slash. An angler tries to deduce the identity of the insect that just went swimming with the fishes. He then offers the trout an artificial fly that resembles the natural, but has a hook in it.

There is, of course, nothing that obliges you to delve into cases of missing insects, and the clues can be complicated. The same mayfly, for example, may disappear at any stage of its life—as a nymph, emerger, juvenile dun, or mature spinner. The trout may also feed on midges, caddisflies, stoneflies, ants, and various other innocents. You could do less thinking for more money elsewhere.

Or you could try a good general fly. Coming up later is a design that may deceive rising trout, even when you do not know which insect they are taking during a complex hatch. It just happens that—for reasons best left to philosophers— many of us anglers enjoy playing detective. Sometimes we even solve our mysteries.

The sleuth in this story knelt by the stream, trying to identify the victims of foul play. Down the current came a tiny mayfly—wings above the water, body still clambering from its nymphal shuck. The emerger drifted into an insect net and posed under a magnifying lens. (Don't laugh at my detective kit. This is a tale in the manner of Sherlock Holmes, not Mike Hammer.)

The insect was an olive, appearing before the hatch was expected. Olive is a handy term for mayflies of the genus *Baetis,* which are small but prolific and widespread. In some streams, olives are to the trout what hamburgers are to human teenagers in the fast-food outlet just up the road.

The obvious fly to try was one imitating an emerging olive dun—the adolescent stage, old enough to leave the nymphal shuck but not ready to start a family. The trout fell for my counterfeit, ran out most of my line upstream, caught the hook in watercress, and twisted free. (At least the fly did not break off. Leader materials are stronger than they were a few years ago, simplifying what used to be an expert's game.)

The next fish was smaller but violent, and on its third jump it lit on the bank, 13 inches of rainbow, fat and trembling.

It would be wrong to deduce, here, that those two trout were feeding *selectively* on emerging olives. To be sure that the evidence would stand up in court, a better detective would have checked the stomach contents of the fish. They could have been eating not only olives but anything else that floated by, except my peacock-herl midge. Trout and anglers often tell different stories about the same event.

What happened later, however, was unmistakable. The duns molted, turning into the adults called spinners, and then mated. Finally, the female spinners returned to the water to lay their eggs, and many of the flies disappeared into excited little rises. (This means that the detective was excited and the fish seemed to get carried away, too.)

I landed a brown and a rainbow, both small, and then cast to another tiny bubble. The rising trout turned out not to be tiny. It tangled the leader in weeds, jumped, and broke off not only the fly but three feet of tippet. By the time Sherlock got back in business, the Tricos were gone and the fish were rising sporadically to something I could not see.

Ants, maybe. Thatch ants, so named for their labor-intensive hills, are under the impression that they own this place, and in fact they have been building it grain by grain over the last ten thousand years, but neither trout nor anglers show any appreciation. (Fly fishing has changed since anglers learned to identify the trout's real prey. The most important spring-creek insects bear little resemblance to our traditional bushy size-14 dry flies.)

I tied an ant imitation to my tippet, and it might have worked if the trout's accomplice had not put in an appearance. Ms. Teal is an actress of modest size and major talent. First she tried to decoy me away from her brood, and I went along with the routine. Then she got carried away by her performance and forgot the ducklings entirely. When her audience—me—fled to a new spot, she flew along and splashed down thirty feet away, uttering piteous quacks and flailing her wings till the only trout in sight stopped rising. I took a hike.

Far upstream in the duck-blind pool, where I refrain from shooting Ms. Teal every October, three trout were acting out a different drama. They streaked around just beneath the surface, displacing more water than a mother duck at her most melodramatic. This was baffling behavior for fish that are ordinarily cautious. There are few minnows in the spring creek, and the usual mayflies and midges do not require an active chase.

Mystery. Solution: a parachute beetle. It probably did not represent what the fish were feeding on, but a fat beetle can sometimes tempt a trout away from its regular food. And after several long casts, the fly lit in front of the closest of the three streaking fish. The rise was violent and so was the fight that followed—a series of leaps that tired the trout before it sought shelter in the weeds. The only trick was to slacken the line with every jump so that the rainbow's weight would not fall on a taut leader.

The fish was fat, shiny, and 18 inches long—enough to make any angler's day. Furthermore, forensic medicine was going to provide a clue that might help me to catch the trout's cronies.

The obvious way to take a stomach sample is to kill the fish, but then I would have been obliged to eat it, and this creek's rainbows taste as strong as they fight. Alternatively, a stomach pump could have been used, but that process makes me feel as guilty as if I had shot Ms. Teal. So I pulled a scoop from my detective kit. The instrument is slender and rounded, and it does the job gently.

The kit had another gadget that came in handy now—a shallow, transparent plastic box. The trick was to put the top part of the stomach contents in the box, add water, and stir till the trout's prey were separated. The mystery insects turned out to be cranefly larvae, big and ugly.

Nothing in my fly box looked exactly like a cranefly larva, but an unweighted hare's nymph came close, and it was big enough to work well on a stouter tippet. The first few casts failed to intercept the next of the trout that cruised the pool. In time, though, the geometry looked right. I lifted my rod tip, pulled the imitation larva past the fish, and watched it take like a tarpon. This rainbow was 19 inches long, but the strong leader allowed me to release it while it still had some jump left.

Three big spring-creek trout do not often make fools of themselves, one after the other, but the sprinting larvae were extraordinarily tempting. The third rainbow was as violent as the other two and a nose longer than 20 inches.

You might say that the day's fishing involved a little bit of everything—hatching nymphs, duns, spinners, even the cranefly Olympics. In fact, however, there was a pattern. All of the trout's victims had died within the top inch of the stream.

For the last century (but not before), we humans have drawn a sharp distinction between dry and wet flies. Trout have not caught up on the literature. They feed wherever their victims are easiest to catch, which in some waters may be near the bottom. In shallow, fertile, weedy streams, however, the surface film traps a concentration of insects. Some of them are in the film and some just below, but all are vulnerable.

Because spring creeks, tailwaters, and chalk streams are so attractive to anglers, many suitable flies are available, including dries, unweighted nymphs, and soft hackles. If you are at a loss for clues, though, consider the parachute fly. On this particular day it worked about half the time.

The advantage of the parachute design is that it transcends the surface film—body down in the trout's world, wing up in the air where you and I can see it. Think of the fly as a nymph with built-in strike indicator, more pleasant to use than a piece of plastic stuck to your leader. And if the parachute deceives even one careless trout for you, you can do your forensic medicine and learn how to catch its smarter relatives.

The point is not to prepare for any particular mystery. You will never have a day exactly like the one described in this tale and neither will I, ever again. Repeating it would be less exciting anyhow. A mystery solved is a mystery no more. The endless satisfaction of fly fishing comes from a drama of suspense played out on the best of stages.

THE DETECTIVE'S KIT

1. Insect net: Stitch fine-meshed netting (available in sewing shops) into the throat of your landing net. An aquarium net works as well but is less handy.

2. Magnifying lens: A collapsible 10-power model is usually enough to identify the genus of a mayfly, and sometimes the species.

3. Magnifying box: On the stream, the most convenient magnifier is a transparent plastic box with a low-power lens built in. Unfortunately, these gadgets can be hard to find. A 10-power folding magnifying glass will usually do the job.

4. Scoop: Plastic or metal models are occasionally available in fly shops, but I prefer mine, which was made from a kitchen spoon by Vincent Marinaro. With hammer, file, and vise with anvil, you could make a similar small scoop— and it does not take a big one to do the job. A semicircular scoop with rounded edges should retrieve a few insects from a sizable fish without damage.

5. Plastic box: Pick one that is white or transparent and small enough to fit in a vest pocket. Remove the top layer of the trout's stomach contents with your scoop, place in the box, add water, and stir to separate.

THE PARACHUTE FLY

Hook: Strong wire, 7–9 mm overall length (sizes 16–20)
Thread: Fine yellow or olive
Wing: Tuft of white calf-tail hair or synthetic yarn
Hackle: Blue dun, wound around base of wing

Tail: Fibers of same hackle
Body: One or two herls from pheasant tail twisted around tying thread and then wound on hook

Change the body from thin pheasant-tail herl to hare's-ear dubbing or fat peacock herl, depending on whether you want to imitate a nymph or dun or beetle. For the wing, use whatever color you find most visible.

Inside the Hidden Hatch

July 4 is the anniversary of two events—one celebrated by fireworks in the evening and the other by headlights before dawn. The Trico hatch is beginning. It has done so at this time for millennia, presumably, but few of us knew it till Vince Marinaro described the "hidden hatch" in print just in time to give purpose to the summer of 1969.

To appreciate the impact, consider how short the season used to seem in the years before Tricos. Back then, Howard T. Walden II wrote that: "There will come an evening in late June or early July when you will know that the best of your sport is over for another year. . . . As you drag your heavy boots or waders up the bank to your waiting car you reflect a little sadly on the evanescence of a trout season."

Marinaro's article doubled the season of heavy eastern hatches. He was by no means the first to see Tricos or to fish imitations of them (as he made clear), but he put them on the map. From 1969 on, we had a new world of fishing to explore. It was not easy at first—the insects seemed too small, too short-lived, too localized, and much too early-rising. Our old ways had to change. Never mind: Now there were trout sipping real mayflies till some time in October.

Later, Montana and Idaho dispelled my notion that the *Tricorythodes* fishing was for easterners. Tricos in the Rockies can be almost too much of a good thing: You hope for a light hatch so that the trout might notice your imitation among a few naturals. What you get, usually, is a day when your wife goes down to the stream for watercress and catches a hundred tiny spinners in her hair.

This is the most abundant, prolonged, and dependable mayfly hatch in the United States. For me it has been the only nationwide hatch, the same from region to region. One caution, however. Scientists and anglers are still discovering the Trico, and sometimes we sound like the blind men groping an elephant: the fellow who found the trunk described a different beast from the one in charge of a leg. Both were right and perhaps all of us are, too, under different conditions that we do not yet understand.

Entomologists, for example, recognize numerous Trico species, including an extra-small one in Montana—but they all look the same to an angler like me. (There is a range of sizes, but all of them can turn up in one hatch and color variations are minor.) Similarly, some writers have described fishing experiences different from mine. I will flag some of the differences without pretending that I can explain them.

Tricos turn up in many streams and some lakes, but most of my experience with the little flies has been in sunny, weedy streams of high fertility. Even in these waters, the flies have been more abundant in some reaches—often the lower ones—than in others.

In most of the trout zone, fortunately, you can drive to the right places instead of taking an airplane; but if the hatch is heavy, roll out of bed in time for the emerging duns. In the East, most anglers arrive too late for anything but the spinner fall.

It does not make sense, but Trico nymphs seem to know about air temperatures. They change into duns before dawn on extra-muggy Pennsylvania nights but not till the middle of cool mornings. How could that information get to insects three feet down in a spring creek with slow-changing temperatures? And in Montana, the hatch may not start till midday.

The spinners are easier to understand. Leigh Perkins reports that they start to fall at an air temperature of 68 degrees. (I have known them to settle for a lower temperature in Montana, but they like warmth when they can get it.)

The mechanics of the hatch are puzzling, too. Some duns emerge while floating down the stream, but I never see enough on the water to account for the hordes in the air an hour or so later. Perhaps some nymphs change underwater, sneaking out ready to fly.

In any case, the scarcity of floating duns provides a way to beat the odds. Trout sipping a few emerging flies as hors d'oeuvres will often take an imitation on the first good cast. It helps to use the right fly, though; at this stage, trout still have time to be selective. You won't find extensive guidance in print because other anglers don't like to get up early any more than I do.

The Barb-Wing Dun comes closer to being a secret weapon than any other Trico in my fly box. Trout may like the design because the pheasant-tail body looks like an emerging fly stuck in the surface film. I like the wing because I can see it. It is made of barbs (fibers) from a glossy white hackle that is wound and then pulled above the hook shank, fanning out into a broad V.

The Barb-Wing is close in structure to both the no-hackle duns and Comparaduns. The hackle is easy to tie in small sizes, more durable than quill wings, and softer in the trout's mouth than deer hair. In Pennsylvania, the Barb-Wing has been catching between three and six fish daily before the spinner fall. The Montana fish are tougher but, relatively, the dun is even more important on cool western mornings; the hatch lasts longer.

The Barb-Wing makes a point that I would ask you to stop and ponder: The best small-fly designs are not just shrunken versions of big ones. This sounds obvious but is, in fact, difficult to grasp. Most of us have a cultural block. We learn to fish with flies of ample size and, when we move to small ones, we carry along a firm notion of what an artificial fly should look like. In the 1960s, for example, I knew that trout taking medium-sized sulphur duns wanted size-18 imitations on 5X tippets. It seemed logical that fish rising for Tricos should want size-24 flies of the same design on 7X monofilament. And that is what I fished. Today, flies like that are still what I see when I go through the bins in fly shops. The folks fishing those flies must be having the same problems I did. No wonder the Tricos have a reputation for difficulty.

Good Trico imitations need not, in fact, be difficult to tie or fish. There are, however, some design problems, so let's construct our Tricos from scratch rather than starting with big, familiar flies and reducing them in scale.

Sizes

The biggest Trico nymphs I have found in both Pennsylvania and Montana measure 7 mm, not counting the tails, and some duns are nearly as big. My imitations of all stages (including the spinners) are tied on hooks measuring 7 or 8 mm overall, including the eye. It's a compromise. The fish may refuse bigger flies, and anything shorter than 7 mm hooks poorly.

The Mustad company uses at least three different scales for trout hooks, and the confusion has increased with the availability of British, Japanese, and French hooks. A size-20 Mustad 94840 hook has about the same length as a size-16 Mustad 3906 (which is a better model for Tricos). The equivalent in Partridge Code A hooks is size 17. The unromantic ruler just keeps on reading 7 mm. Recommendation: Get a small metric ruler and forget the sizes you read on boxes.

Wing Flies

Whether we photograph mayflies or bathing suits, we prefer models with perfect bodies; but when female Trico spinners have laid their eggs and fallen spent in the stream, there is not much body left. I used too much film trying to photograph mayflies without makeup as they floated naturally down the stream, and they were nothing that would sell calendars.

Trico wings, on the other hand, hold their shape and become the most visible feature of the spent flies, especially when you look up through the water. Try it with a glass pie dish. The spent wings get caught in the surface film and create a striking light pattern. Next, try thinking of spinner imitations as wing flies, not body flies. It is another one of those things that are culturally difficult.

THE WEAKEST LINK

With leader materials stronger than they used to be, hooks are sometimes the weakest links in our tackle. Mustad 948-series hooks are springy and have poor hooking geometry in the small sizes. In size 20, the 94840 may open far enough to lose a trout if the hook is caught in the trout's mouth by the point only. A hook that has fully penetrated will take a stronger pull.

Some of the new Japanese hooks (available in a confusing variety of brands) are stronger and have better shapes in the small sizes.

The strength problem is not critical in most eastern waters, but for heavy Montana trout in weedy streams, try the Partridge Code A. Romantics will be encouraged to find that it is an old design, apparently identical to the Hardy hook that Americans liked early in the twentieth century. (Check Preston Jennings's book.) By comparison with the size-20 Mustad, the size-17 Partridge has the same length and is almost twice as strong, testing at $2\frac{3}{4}$ pounds. It also has 40 percent more gape, which helps to get the fly stuck in the trout in the first place. For best hooking geometry, it is important to get the down-eyed version.

This hook seems heavy to most anglers today. You may be surprised, however, to find that weight is less of a problem in small flies. Try this experiment: Place a small, bare hook on your fingertip and immerse your finger in a pan of water. The hook will float readily in the surface tension. A medium size will also float, but with more difficulty. A big streamer hook will not float at all.

The smaller the fly, then, the easier it is to get away with a relatively stout hook. It's counterintuitive but it works. The small, strong, wide-gape hooks also seem to "anchor" the fly in the surface film, resisting drag.

THE SPINNER GLUT

There is a Pennsylvania spring creek in which, as far as I can tell, the Trout eat virtually nothing but Tricos from the Fourth of July till late September. The stream has a reputation for difficulty—and no wonder. Most anglers arrive after the hatch is over for the day.

The feeding frenzy comes when the Tricos are in their final spinner stage. A trout will gobble spinners till his stomach is stuffed like a black sausage. Then he will eat till the flies he started with an hour earlier are forced out his vent. This translates into hundreds of rises, during any one of which he might take an artificial fly—but probably won't. The odds are against us fishermen. We get frantic, too, given so many missed opportunities.

The logical assumption is that the trout is selective, and the logical response is to make the flies we offer him more realistic. Further, we like to define realism in terms of color. For a time I tried to make my female spinners prettier, with black thoraxes, green-tinged white abdomens, pale dun wings, and wispy hooks. Every one of my flies rose trout, which seemed to show that I was doing something right.

But then, by way of experiment, I tried some improbable imitations of small beetles and found that they worked about as well as my pretty Tricos. And in Montana, my friends started using small Renegades.

On a difficult spring creek that I know well, one of the best fishermen is Glenn Brackett—and last time I checked, he had a little doodad with a red body on his line. The only thing most of the best anglers had in common was that they had drifted away from ultrasmall hooks.

Perhaps the situation is different on streams with sparse spinner falls. The ones I fish have gluts, and during them the trout are not, it turns out, very selective. They do not have time to be. They insist that the fly behave correctly (floating without drag and low in the surface film). The size cannot be much too large. Sometimes I fancy that a broad wing silhouette helps a little (which could explain the success of the Renegade). But I have not been able to demonstrate color selectivity to spinners.

Of course, that's only the fish's point of view. You, the angler, need three things in addition to good hooking ability:

- Good flotation. You must make many accurate casts (short ones if possible) over gobbling fish, without wasting time false casting or greasing your fly.
- Durability. The fly should stay in shape for the whole orgy so that you don't waste time preening and changing it.
- Visibility. You need to know when the trout takes your fly as opposed to one of the gross of naturals floating nearby.

Let's start by rejecting all flies that are difficult to see on the water. Out goes any design that looks like a proper spent spinner to humans—including all those pretty ones with spent (horizontal) wings of hackle fibers. Ant imitations are equally hard to see and even worse for flotation.

Parachute flies are visible because their horizontal wing is usually wrapped around a vertical post, and brilliant synthetic-fiber posts are very visible indeed. They are ugly (my bias), but trout have no objections.

Perhaps we can improve a little on the flotation and durability of parachute flies without losing visibility. A white, shiny hackle is easy to see, so let's start with that. Let's wind it over the front two-thirds of the hook for a broad wing silhouette, adding a widespread V-tail for additional flotation. Let's put a wisp of dubbing on the thread and wind the body forward *over* the hackle to secure it. Then let's clip the hackle flat on the bottom for low flotation. Finally, let's seal head, tail, and hackle with tiny drops of penetrating rod varnish, not cement. This fly won't get out of shape in a hurry. Mind you, I'm not saying that the trout like it better than any other—just that they like it as well, and I can fish it better. It helps in playing the odds.

The nymphs make a shorter story. Ernest Schwiebert, Al Caucci, and Bob Nastasi describe Trico nymphs as important, but I find few in trout stomachs. (Another difference in streams, perhaps.) And artificial nymphs don't catch much for me at the beginning of the hatch. They do, however, pick up the occasional fish looking for stragglers at the end. The trick is to use a nymph that fishes just under the surface, where you can see a trout rise. The Invisible-Hackle Nymph has some helpful behavior designed in: A couple of turns of stiff, translucent hackle help the fly land gently and sink slowly. You can often see trout rising a little for the nymph.

LEADERS

We used to think of extra-fine tippets as sporting, but when we used them, we had to play sizable trout to exhaustion. Today, most of us release most of our fish, and a strong tippet helps to get them in without exhausting their stores of energy.

Fortunately, leader materials have become stronger. An .005-inch tippet is now reliable for Pennsylvania trout, and even for spring-creek fish in Montana early in the season. When weeds grow thick, an .006-inch tippet helps to net a heavy trout before it buries itself in the weeds. But again, the label may not be accurate. You can count on a micrometer.

Measuring things is not as poetic as fishing a size-24 fly on a 7X leader. That's a pity, because you and I are the last of the romantics. We love X-rated tippets and zinfandel and bamboo rods and ladies who patch our fishing pants with blue-denim hearts. Too bad the stupid fish don't appreciate us.

The other day a Montana trout gobbling Trico spinners turned out to be a nose longer than 20 inches. I'd have changed the tippet if I'd known, but the new .004 inch-stuff held. A fly the size of a mosquito looked ridiculous in the jaws of a fish that should have been feeding on the muskrat hatch.

Vince Marinaro would have liked that brown. He wrote that the biggest wild fish he'd landed on a Trico was 18 inches long. Vince wanted to come to Montana when we talked about the good browns feeding on Tricos, but he would not get in an airplane and the passenger trains had been discontinued.

He didn't miss much, really: The hidden hatch is not for big fish, even if a big one forgets himself on occasion. Tricos are small flies, big hatches, and serious fishing. You appreciate all of those things most near home, in the months when you thought the fun was over.

DRESSINGS FOR TRICO DUN, SPINNER, AND NYMPH IMITATIONS

Hook: 7 or 8 mm overall length, strong wire
Cement: Penetrating rod varnish instead of regular cement.
(Allow to dry overnight.)

BARB-WING DUN

Thread: Pale green or yellow.
Tail: Pale hackle fibers, about 7 mm long, in broad V.
Wing: White hackle, about 9 mm in length of barb. Wind in normal fashion, then pull into an upright V-shaped wing fanning out over about 120 degrees. Secure with figure-8 wraps of tying silk under shank of hook. Tie wing before body.
Body: Two pheasant-tail herls spun around waxed tying thread, then wound sparsely. Take a figure-8 wrap under the wings to form broad thorax.

WING-FLY SPINNER

Thread: Black.
Tail: Dun hackle barbs, about 10 mm in length,

spread into broad V.

Wing: Shiny, stiff white hackle wound over front two-thirds of hook shank. Fiber length about 5 mm. Trim bottom of hackle after body is wound.

Body: Wind tying thread (lightly dubbed with black fur) through the hackle to reinforce it. The body is on top of the hackle.

INVISIBLE-HACKLE NYMPH

Thread: Same as dun.

Body: Same materials as dun, but form a small thorax bulge behind the hackle.

Tail: Allow tips of body herls to protrude about 5 mm.

Hackle: Two wraps of watery blue dun cock's hackle, barb length about 4 mm.

Sunbeams

You would not notice these tiny mayflies if they had died as nature intended. They were meant to live three hundred and sixty-four days in river-bottom muck, then shed their nymphal husks, dance in the dawn sky, and lay their eggs on a stream's silver surface. Trout were meant to sip the spent dancers. You were meant to cast a sunbeam fly and catch a trout fat as summer.

A spider spoiled the show. Spun a web in streamside willows; caught black ardent males and female mayflies swollen with eggs. How can this waste of beauty and protein fit nature's plan?

Because there is no plan, and no nature either, except as that which is not human. There is just life—great and small, lovely and ugly, abundant and wasteful and never long enough.

PART FOUR

Wild Fish

Rainbow Rising

*I*t's about time. All winter you have been tying flies for this hatch and now here it is and you are surrounded by feeding trout and you are going to catch them all, starting with the biggest.

Its silver flank rolls in the current. You cast a skittering sedge and give it a twitch. The trout rolls again, but your fly is still on the water, rocking in the ripples of the rise. So forget the fast food. Try a partridge-hackle emerger.

Well, maybe not. Maybe that old rainbow was chasing a caddis pupa. Cast a bead-head imitation and let it sink and then lift it in front of the fish. And don't forget to breathe.

He missed! Or maybe that fussy rainbow ignored your fly and took one of the real insects.

Never mind: the caddisflies love you. Look at the pretty green egg sacs they have laid on your waders, and draw a deep breath.

Well, spit it out. You picked a bad time to hyperventilate. With ten thousand flies in the air, you've got to keep your mouth shut.

Spring Fever

In the spring, some idiot wrote, a young man's fancy turns to love. The author was confusing humans with pandas, which have a mating season. We don't. If we did, however, we would postpone it till July. In the spring, young men (and some older ones) turn to trout brooks and brook trout.

One day last May, therefore, I was standing on the Blue Ridge, shading my eyes, and looking down at Dogwood Run. It was six miles distant and sixteen hundred feet lower in elevation, wedged between two mountains turning green. I was thinking how much I would enjoy fishing the stream, and how much I would not enjoy the hike back uphill. No sensible person would undertake such a march for a little fish.

(But spring fever is a kind of energy. It is released by the sun, then absorbed by maple sap, wild garlic, and me. The best place to cool off is a trout stream. Dogwood Run is as cool as they get.)

In a couple of hours I reached the water, pulled the hip boots from my backpack, put them on, strung up my rod, and walked another mile downstream. I knew just where to go. Once I had lived near here, in our nation's capital, and Dogwood Run became my oasis in the Great American Desert—spared from fishing pressure because it was hard to reach. It was moody, though, and sometimes it sent me puffing back up the trail without trout, which made me love them all the more.

(The Great American Desert is another of those topics on which there has been confusion. It used to be a large unpopulated area in the middle of our continent, but in this century it has become the suburbs, where it is made up of shopping malls, roads between shopping malls, and cars driving to shopping malls with their air conditioners on.)

At the good pool below a cliff, I dropped to my knees and sneaked within range. A sidearm cast hid my rod from any trout that might be watching. The little fly lit twenty feet upstream and floated back toward me, lazy, as I lifted the rod and kept most of the line off the water. A trout appeared under the fly, drifted with it for a second, and sucked it down just like that: one cast, one rise, one fish on the hook. Too good to be true.

This, however, seemed too big to be a brook trout. Maybe some criminal had polluted my stream with another species. I jumped to my feet and ran downstream to keep the angle of pull from changing. The trout rolled on the surface. It was the real thing.

(Once, in West Africa, I had caught a 200-pound fish of less magnitude, but what would you expect? That was only a tarpon.)

Allow me to apologize for suggesting, a few miles back, that Dogwood Run has small trout. One of the special virtues of brook trout is that they get big faster than other fish. An 8-inch rainbow trout, for example, is dinky, but an 8-inch brook trout is a weighty matter. A 200-pound tarpon looks big but has less gravity than the 11-inch brook trout that splashed in my net on Dogwood Run.

I released the big trout. Do not assume, however, that I was making a statement. (Fly fishermen are perfect in most other respects but fond of statements.) I would have savored this trophy for dinner if my motel's restaurant had been willing to cook it, but I had inquired and found that the chef had never cooked anything unfrozen and was not about to start.

(He did not know what he was missing. Brook trout are more succulent than steak, more delicate than caviar, more supportive than Mother's Thanksgiving turkey. Brook trout are prolific, too. You may eat them occasionally without guilt.)

This trout gave me the nourishment I needed anyhow. As I released it and climbed out of the stream, several trilliums burst through the soil, a dogwood tree rushed into blossom, and a pair of mallards flew from the pool above me. Dogwood Run is poor duck habitat, so I supposed that they had flown in to admire the trout, like me.

(Brook trout are the most beautiful of fish. I expect no argument on that subject, but tell me: Are they beautiful because they live in such places or are the places beautiful because they harbor such trout?)

The next pool upstream was spread more widely, but the water at its head curved around three scattered granite boulders and dug deep pockets in their lee. I fished the first two boulders carefully but found no fish around them. One, however, was located in such a way that I could cast my line over it and let the fly drop below the third boulder, just upstream. With no line dragging, the fly lit and eddied like a natural insect.

A trout rose, purposefully but without commotion, as brook trout do when they are big enough to have chased their competition from a pool. This one took the fly with confidence. It then fought with more dignity than me, seeking refuge under all three of the boulders without success. It was almost as big as my first, 10 inches plus.

I give you these statistics in order to brag convincingly. Some people will tell you that the point of fishing is to escape from daily worries, so if the fish do not cooperate, who cares? (I care.) People say, too, that fishing is just an excuse to get out and admire nature. (But I don't want to be a spectator. I want to play the game.)

The passion for brook trout is not rational. If it made sense, it would not be passion, would it? It is, however, widespread. You can prove this to yourself by going into any tackle shop and asking for directions to some good trout fishing in the area. The friendly fellow behind the counter will send you to a river with brown trout or rainbows. Ask him, then, if he could direct you to a good stream for brookies. Well, gee, no—you've got him stumped there. By a remarkable coincidence, every sporting-goods store in America just happens to be located in a region that has no brook trout within range of the owner's recollection.

You might conclude that the species is scarce. On the contrary, it is widespread and abundant. Passion, however, is private. A fellow who would publicize a brook-trout stream would write his girlfriend's number on the wall of a phone booth.

(Listen carefully, now, and I'll tell you once how to find Dogwood Run. You start in Maine and drive halfway to Georgia. You park under a pine tree, leave a note in your car assuring your wife that you died happy, and walk as far as you can, plus another mile. You're there.)

Above the Three-Rock Pool was a long, shallow, sunny riffle—the kind of place that produces food for trout—and above the riffle was a pool that curved to the left under a deep bank. Where brush shaded the stream, a trout rose twice. I could see no insects on the water and guessed that beetles had fallen from the overhanging vegetation. They had been crawling across the trail, plump insects the color of bronze peacock herl, and I knew from the old days that trout fed on them every spring.

Catching this rising trout took no great skill, but I deserved it, having fished the Appalachians for many whole seasons without a trophy, which is to say a brook trout more than 10 inches in length. This one was fully 11, as big as my first of the day. With three great fish in a row, I could reasonably conclude that my totem trout were welcoming me back.

(I am happy for friends who go to Alaska for vast fish of several kinds, sparing my hidden brook-trout waters. But there is a place in Canada where big brook trout still rise for mayflies, and maybe I'll find a way to get there. A fish of 14 pounds, 9 ounces would be a record, best of the last, bigger by an ounce than a brook trout caught in the Nipigon River in 1916. Trout and I would both become immortal.)

The sky went cloudy in the afternoon, and I imagined myself slogging out of Dogwood Run in the rain. Gusts blew upstream, darkening the water, blowing the tops off miniature whitecaps. Wait: Some of those splashes were made by fish working a hatch of big mayflies.

I changed to a Quill Gordon and let the wind dap it over the trout. One rose and missed the bouncing fly. I saw that the fish was of no great size and moved upstream. A better fish took with a splash, felt the hook, ran upstream into the shallows, and jumped—a low jump but a real one, arching over the water. Brook trout do that on a few streams. This fish was 12 inches long, my best from the Appalachians for twenty years.

Dogwood Run was the kind of place that ghosts like, intimate as the cabins that mountain people used to build on its banks. Curves in the stream gave views only of woods and hills. I could believe, for a time, that the whole world was like this.

(Once I lived in a Rip Van Winkle house that had an attic for playing and a hideaway under the stairs. These places were fun because they were secret. Dogwood Run had clear water too, and trout cozy between cities. It was the secret, maybe, that brought me all the way back here from Montana. Home is where the brook trout hide.)

The stream went to sleep, then, or at least its trout did, and in two hours I caught only three fingerlings. I was fishing hard, too, creeping on my knees to the best places, floating my fly like a desperate beetle. Then I switched to a nymph and fished it ticking along the bottom. Nothing took it. I squinted my eyes red and saw only a smallmouth bass, which worried me. Bass are not native here, and they might bother my brook trout.

(I deplore the disappearance of so many strains of native trout in the West, pushed to extinction by brook trout introduced from the East. I don't stop at deploring, either. I do my best to keep those brook trout under control, fishing for them through rain and cold and mosquitoes.)

I did not deserve any more trout from Dogwood Run, but I was not ready for the return to civilization, so I hiked up to the Split-Rock Pool, an old favorite just below the falls. The little fly floated lonely as an asteroid, and a brookie appeared in the magical way of its kind, coming from nowhere, pulled by some celestial gravity. It orbited for a light-year, fins quivering. When it took the fly, the movement was so quick that I saw only an aurora of light and color.

I was grateful to whoever let me watch this all by myself. Perhaps I would just keep on fishing forever.

The Brown Trout and the
Great Tradition

There is in fly fishing a great tradition, and it evolved around a peculiar quarry called the brown trout. Most of us, by now, owe our angling attitudes to that trout and tradition. We Americans are ambivalent about traditions; we may be unaware that the brown trout shaped us; we seldom make it a sentimental favorite like the native brook trout. But the brown informs us constantly.

Brown. One knows, right away, that such a name comes from long ago and far away. If we were doing it now, we would want a designer label—something with glitter, pugnacity, syllables. Golden, perhaps, or cutthroat, or rainbow. But the brown is the original trout, and it does not need to prove anything. Describing it as a fish is like calling wheat a grass—true, but not much of the story. Our ancestors discovered both grain and trout upon leaving the Garden of Eden, give or take a few centuries, and each discovery started something of consequence. I propose to look at what the brown trout did to us: its influence, not its fishness.

Three of the brown's oddities help to explain its effect on us, the anglers.

- First, the rise: The trout feeds near the surface of the water, with me watching, and draws me in with the fly.
- Second, selectivity: The brown trout keeps on taking natural flies but rejects my imitations of them, making the choice with a logic that I think I can understand.
- Third, time: Trout and I have been doing this for a lot of centuries, recording what we have learned in genes and books.

Getting a Rise Out of Him

What we humans call the surface of the water is, for a fish, the surface of the air. Either way, it is the boundary between worlds, important to the residents of both and difficult to cross for either. Insects coming from both directions get stuck. Many fish have learned to feed on the insects, especially in America. In the old-world streams where trout and man first met each other, however, the brown trout (in my experience) rises more frequently than other fish of equal size—members of the carp family, mostly, with salmon, grayling, and pike in some streams. The brown is also more prized as food than any other river fish except the salmon. This trout has therefore evolved under the dual handicaps of desirability and visibility. In order to survive, it had to be clever, which in the oldest sense means (according to my dictionary) "expert to seize, dexterous."

As to what the trout eats, you may be aware by now (if you read the literature) that nymphs make up 80 percent of the diet. Or maybe it's 90 percent. Anyhow, most of what a trout eats is nymphs and you ought to be using one.

As bromides go, this one is instructive for three reasons.

First, it has been repeated not only by purveyors of nymphs but also by writers from whom readers expect independent, accurate information.

Second, the figures are implausible at first glance. A trout getting 80 percent of its diet from nymphs would have to pass up other food that is widely available in streams—including adult aquatic insects of all kinds, terrestrial insects, scuds, snails, sow bugs, crayfish, minnows, the larvae and pupae of caddisflies and midges, and so on.

Third, this bit of fishy wisdom can be traced to its source without much effort. (Small errors can be hard to run down, in a sport as old as fly fishing, but a real whopper is likely to have been invented only once.)

In this case, the author was Edward R. Hewitt, who did everything on a larger-than-life scale. In two books (the first in 1934), he cited a finding that "over 80 percent of the trout food consisted of nymphs." Fortunately, he gave his source of information—unlike some of his successors. The research on which he drew was done at Cornell University by Paul R. Needham, who surveyed brook, brown, and rainbow trout in New York streams.

I went back to Needham's research and found that mayfly nymphs made up about 33 percent of the food items of the trout surveyed. Stonefly nymphs made up another 1 percent.

In the winter 1991 issue of *Trout* magazine, Robert J. Behnke also compared Hewitt's statement to the original Needham research. "A case could be made from Needham's data," Behnke said, "that dry-fly fishing should be more effective than nymph fishing." Behnke further mentioned research by Needham—this time in California—on a trout population that got 10 percent of its food from nymphs.

On the stream, we are not helped much by generalities anyhow. We play a real-life detective game: finding out where a trout is feeding, and on what, and then trying to offer a fly with the right behavior, size, shape, and color. Like the games in mystery books, this one can be a matter of life and death for one of the actors.

There is some hard information. A study of Spruce Creek brown trout by Robert A. Bachman found that some 7 to 13 percent of "feeding events" took place on the bottom of the stream. The rest of the events were divided about equally between surface and midwater. Many nymphs and pupae were present on the bottom, but they were hard to see, and many were hidden in spaces between rocks. Food items in "the drift," on the other hand, were silhouetted against the sky, making them easier to see.

This research does not necessarily apply to other waters or species. It does describe a kind of brown-trout behavior that fly fishermen were, according to Ælian, already exploiting in the third century.

For the most part, fly fishing evolved around the rise. The books seem clear on this point, once you learn to read them. You have to avoid getting sidetracked by a fascinating old debate on the origins of dry-fly fishing. Jack Heddon in England and Paul Schullery here have helped to clear up the confusion, which is not to say that either would agree with me. My conclusion is that the dry fly originated in 1886, precisely. In that year a gentleman named Frederic M. Halford wrote a book providing the necessary mythology. There was no dry-fly fishing before Halford. There was no Greece before Homer. There were, of course, Greek-speaking people before Homer, and some of them were probably fishing for brown trout with floating flies, but back then nobody knew what he was doing.

Now that we all know what we're doing, it is difficult to pose questions that would have made sense to our ignorant ancestors. If, however, you had asked a good early angler something simple—such as whether his flies ever floated—he would have said that, yes, of course they did: What else would a fly do before it soaked up water? He might have added that floating flies were good for fooling a difficult trout. After a few casts, however, the flies would sink, but the rate of sinking would be slow, and by control of the line, the angler could keep them near enough to the surface that he could see trout rising for them. The flies typically imitated surface insects (as North Country wet flies still do).

If you were able to pursue this conversation, you might conclude that our early trout fisherman did not see much difference between "wet" and "dry." He would, however, have seen a difference between fly fishing (near the surface) and something else: bait, for example, or what Hewett Wheatley, in 1849, described as "artificial Grub-fishing." We would now call it fishing with a weighted nymph. Wheatley even used a strike indicator, which he called a float. He was a good fisherman, but his euphemisms needed work.

By the late nineteenth century, anglers had means of keeping flies afloat without resorting to dapping, cross-lines, cork bodies, and so on. The improved equipment included stiffer split-bamboo rods, greased silk lines, new fly designs, and fly flotants, more or less in that order. New gear made it possible for Halford to bestow the myth. A few decades later we had thin synthetic leaders, sinking lines, and graphite rods, which made it easier to fish deep. There were curmudgeons who said that this wasn't fly fishing, but it caught trout and humans. Fly fishermen must have decided that the psychic rewards were, at least, greater than those of spinning with metal lures.

We have made good use of our technology. There is a boom in dry-fly fishing, and deep fishing, though still short of myth, is also catching plenty of trout.

The odd thing is that few of us are still competent with the old midwater flies, which have the best myths in the sport. We could use lessons from an angler like the Portuguese friend who visited me last summer. Adriano does not know enough English to read the glories of angling literature, but he is a product of the great tradition nevertheless. He fished a cast of small wet flies in the old-world way: upstream, near the surface, and with just enough drag to keep track of them.

The trout rose as they have for centuries.

THE FISH THAT CHOOSES

Half the fun of fishing for rising trout is seeing the object of your lust right there, playing catch-me-if-you-can. The other half is discovering that you can't. When you begin to think that you have the hang of it, you find a more desirable trout. There is always a fish somewhere upstream that you are not good enough to fool. It is likely to be a brown.

I surmise that we taught trout to cope by exaggerating a natural characteristic, in much the same way that we taught the pointing dog to exaggerate the wolf's pause before pouncing. Even wilderness trout are wary at the top of a stream; they know that they are vulnerable, up there, to natural predators. The air/water interface is no more user-friendly for trout than for insects. We added a complication when we made fake flies that look like real ones. Some trout have become good at telling the difference. Today we call them selective.

All of the insect-eating trout seem to have a genetic potential for selectivity. It happens that the most selective fish I found in one recent season were cutthroats rising for something very small in the Yellowstone River. Day in and day out, however, most of us find that brown trout are the best at eating real insects while rejecting fakes. It is not likely to be a coincidence that the trout which has known us longest is the most careful of the food he eats.

We call this habit selectivity, and I have elsewhere called it "the best thing about trout." It has certainly been the best thing for people who write books about trout. Perhaps not even browns are quite as discriminating as we anglers like to think, but they reject our flies often enough to have appealed to writers from Ælian to Zern.

THE GREAT TRADITION

Even a fish as unusual as the brown trout could not, of itself, create a tradition; traditions are always human. This one took shape in Britain, flowed to the early colonies with the English language, and has since colonized most of the trout-fishing world. Today American, Argentine, Australian, Danish, Dutch, and South African fly fishermen are more remarkable for the assumptions they share than for the few on which they differ.

About now, however, we need to pause for a cooldown. A woolly old natural philosopher named Izaak Walton portrayed anglers as gentle and uncontentious. This shows how little he knew about fly fishermen. We are a volatile tribe, quick to boil with indignation, or at least simmer with giggles, and in either case I may already have rattled someone's cage by writing about rising trout and selectivity.

Tradition is even more dangerous. We normally call on it only to create atmosphere, or to sanctify what we mean to do anyhow. We adore tradition at a fairy-tale level, like royalty, but do not invite it to go fishing. Unlike royalty, tradition comes along uninvited.

I may get in less trouble if I make clear that I am not trying to be a historian. Historians are obliged to record things that mattered once, whether there were consequences or not. Like fly fishermen, too, historians must take an interest in small things, and some take refuge in them. The writers mentioned here have broader visions; look to them for your history.

My subject is the way we fish today, and why: origins, not history. Why do Hisatsugu Haneda, Preben Torp Jacobsen, and (probably) you share an attitude toward fly fishing—an attitude that did not originate in any of our countries? It must have taken a powerful idea to convert the world.

The indisputably great thing about the great tradition is the number of books it has produced. I would not care to argue that the sport (as opposed to the literature) of trout fishing is greater than, for example, the sport of pheasant hunting. If you get through many catalogs of old sporting books, however, you will note that fly-fishing titles are the most abundant and often the most expensive. Why?

The sport has claimed two dimensions: art and science. Art is the human side. It includes skill and aesthetics and tackle. These can get complicated if we wish, as we usually do. Rods, reels, and (especially) flies are such appealing crafts that they are collected even by nonanglers. The art of fly fishing accounts for many of its books. Other sports, however, have similar books and as much gear. Hunting has dogs and guns. Baseball fans collect even more useless facts than anglers.

The science of angling is different in that it aims at trout, not humans. Science is another word for the ancient detective game played out between man and nature. The most unusual thing about fly fishing is the depth of these inquiries. People involved in other sports have inquiring minds, too (being often the same people), but they rarely have as much to inquire about. New angling entomologies—books describing the insects that trout eat and ways to imitate them on a hook—are being published every year. Compare this with the scarcity of writing on the pheasant, which came to America at the same time as the brown trout and became, perhaps, equally popular. I love them both but could not write a book on the food of the pheasant.

The difference is science. Pheasant hunting takes art but not much science. With trout, when you have found your quarry you must still persuade it to eat. At worst, or best, it may be selective, in which case you have to see what kind of insect it is taking and imitate nature on a hook. Some anglers catch real flies in nets and then tie imitations, but I don't suppose that most of us do this often. We may let others do the science for us, or we may learn from experience that a size-16 Adams looks like something hatching in this particular creek on a cloudy-warm day in May. Science does not have to be more than a careful way of seeing nature.

Science accounts for much writing about fishing, but it is never pure science; not always good science, either. John Gierach notes that our knowledge "draws heavily on science, especially the easygoing, slightly bemused, English-style naturalism of the last century, but it periodically leaves the bare facts behind to take long voyages into anthropomorphism and sheer poetry."

Time has a way of sorting out the books. Check the prices of early editions by Aldam, Davy, Edmonds & Lee, Flick, Halford, Harding, Harris, Jennings, Mackintosh, Marinaro, Mottram, Pritt, Pulman, Ronalds, Sawyer, Scotcher, Shipley, Skues, Theakston, Wade, and Woolley. This is a very short list of authors who are safely deceased but still modern. They have the art, some of them, but they also come close to a dictionary definition of science: "The observation, identification, description, experimental investigation, and theoretical explanation of natural phenomena." There is not as much of this in other sports, and I am not sure that there is anywhere else in literature such a mixture of art and science. Usually the artists look down on the scientists, who are not even aware of the artists. Both of them find fishing literature odd.

Next I have to use a dirty word. Elitism. Sorry. The E-word used to be naughty but nice, and nowadays it's not even nice, which means that we yearn for it more than ever. Once we could at least recognize the devil's work when we saw it. Then (in the 1960s, if memory serves) the elites went undercover. All people and all things became equally good. A professor of biology was no longer to be considered a higher product of evolution than, for example, a mite living on his skin. Each was equally adapted to its niche and, indeed, while the mite might start an itch in the niche, no mite had ever started a war.

If you are too young to recall what happened next, here is a multiple-choice quiz. With anglers free to do their own thing, which fish did they do it to?

   (a) Catfish, using trot lines baited with green chick-
      en gizzards
   (b) Bluegills, using hooks baited with red flannel
      from old long johns
   (c) The most discriminating of trout, using artificial
      flies that represent insects with Latin names

Do you wonder what American fishermen were like in those old, upside-down times when they wanted to be elitist but had no brown trout? Well, their yearnings become clear in 202 letters that they sent to Mary Orvis Marbury in the 1880s. These have been reprinted in a beautiful book: *Favorite Flies and Their Histories*. To flip its pages is to travel to a better place—a country of fragrant streams and big brook trout. I have just traveled through my reprint with a pencil.

Mary Orvis Marbury was a good editor, and few of her contributors, especially from Pennsylvania, seem to have been skilled fishermen. Most sound as if they would not catch much a century later. They rarely describe their method of stream fishing, perhaps assuming that there was only one: across and down with a team of big, fancy wet flies. Of course, those were primitive times. Or were they? The trout and the streams were clearly more innocent, but the letters inclined to the highfalutin.

These American anglers were Victorian. They debated trivia like the killing color for a fly but, on difficult topics, invoked the founding fathers—all British. I started to count the patterns of American origin but was unable, in many cases, to decide where the dividing line should be drawn. Two "hackles" of deer hair seemed original. Most of the other patterns were copies of copies of old-world originals, changing only colors. The originals had not been based on American nature, and the derivatives became even more stiff, stylized, gorgeous—as close to decadence as to innocence. Charles Dudley Warner (one of the contributors) wrote that "The trout fly is a 'conventionalized' creation, as we say of ornamentation. The theory is that, fly-fishing being a high art, the fly must not be a tame imitation of nature, but an artistic suggestion of it."

The ornaments burned brightly and quickly. None of them seem widely used, now, in the original wet-fly form. (The Royal Coachman has prospered by turning into a dry fly.) But I do not mean to suggest that the century-old flies were worse, in some absolute way, than modern ones. You have to decide whether flies should be designed to please trout or people. If people, then the old flies were as good as the new—better, by Charles Dudley Warner's standard of artistic ornamentation. The 1880s flies would have taken more skill to tie than most on the market today. They were prettier, too, and they meant as much to their users.

To the extent that fishing has to do with catching clever trout, however, we tie better flies today. Fly fishing returned to its natural sources when the fishing got tough. We humans might have continued to prefer Charles Dudley Warner's "high art," but the brown trout would not have it. And when we Americans learned how to fish for the new species, original books started to blossom: La Branche's, Hewitt's, Jennings's. An imported fish continues to encourage American originality, which may not be as strange as it sounds. The brown trout has now evolved in this country for at least twice as many generations as any angling writer.

The big change in our fishing coincided with the naturalization of the brown trout, but it would be wrong to credit, or blame, just the fish. The nation got older, richer, more populous, more interested in recreation. The streams deteriorated. The native trout retreated, adapted, or both. Statistically, they are still easier to catch, but individually they can be just as tough. In time the natives might have forced us to pay more attention to nature's doings. The time was not granted.

In a few decades after Mary Orvis Marbury's book, we learned how to catch a different trout. It gave us the mystery we needed for good detective stories. It taught us to design flies for fish, not people. It immersed us in the quizzical relationship with nature that makes this sport different from others.

Perhaps no fish can be said to think. The brown trout, at least, made *us* think.

Scoring

Lee Wulff was ahead of his time when he wrote, in 1939, that "a game fish is too valuable to be caught only once." Most anglers in those days killed every trout they could catch, then called on the government to stock more. The fishing got worse despite the hatcheries' best efforts. Research has since shown that tame fish can stress wild, stream-bred trout, doing more harm than good to a fishery.

Today, most anglers release much of their catch, and wild populations are thriving. What's more, high-quality fishing in my part of the trout belt has made the new economy more prosperous than the old, with guides, shops, realtors, and builders working overtime. Elsewhere in the nation, mean- while, the rust belt is rusting, inner cities are in trouble, and even the malls are losing customers. The shop-till-you-drop crowd has discovered fly fishing.

You will have noticed that Lee Wulff sold catch-and-release management with the word "valuable," and my language has also come from the marketplace, to this point. No apology. The market can be—must be—an ally of nature. The value of the trout's pretty spotted skin has already helped us humans to save its streams.

If each fish and each angler is part of an economic resource, however, each is also an individual, and the individuals have gone through something that I had not foreseen. Two events on the same day opened my eyes.

The first jolt came when I landed a feeble rainbow with fungus on its sides and fresh scars on its mouth. Later on, I saw another discolored fish and one that was half blind. My last trout of the day had a section of loose gill. Those fish were, to be sure, a minority in a healthy population. Their habitat was a popular spring creek—the kind where every rise is likely to be covered by a dry fly or nymph.

The second eye-opener came that evening, as we fisherfolk pulled off our waders. One young man reported that he had averaged four trout per hour—a good score, he thought, but not fabulous. He would have to do twice as well to achieve a "hundred-trout day." He would release all his fish, of course. He had already released himself. His sport was immaculately conceived, free from guilt.

Mine was not. An older friend named Vincent Marinaro had put the remorse back in my fishing a decade earlier, when I was returning a trout to the stream despite a red stain left by my hook. I remember what Vince said, blunt and final: "Fishing is a blood sport."

It has been a blood sport forever. Some few million years ago, one of our ancestors—yours and mine—stuck a spear in the meatiest prey around. The fishhook took longer to perfect but, in the fifteenth century, a treatise on angling was spliced onto a hunting book, as if an afterthought.

Hunting and fishing are still the same sport at core, and letting your prey go is always an alternative. Perhaps, for example, you have rested crosshairs on a buck's brisket and decided not to pull the trigger. That deer got off lightly, by comparison to a hooked trout.

A biologist tells me that an angler who releases many fish "may be doing a lot more damage than the guy who catches his two trout and goes home." The mortality ranges from negligible, at low temperatures, to 10 percent when the water warms. Economically speaking, most fish populations can sustain such a harvest. Ethically speaking, however, there is no such thing as no-kill fishing.

My focus, remember, has shifted from populations to individuals. Individual humans have always hunted individual prey—deer and fish and woolly mammoths—but until recently served them for dinner. This is the first century in which some of us (in the supermarket nations, at least) can afford to wash our hands of bloody old nature.

We still live on other life, though. Always have, always will. If you prefer, take Genesis as the authority for your diet, instead of evolution. Or read the great myths, which provide clear and compelling guidance.

The "basic hunting myth is a kind of covenant between the animal world and the human world," says Joseph Campbell in *The Power of Myth*. Hunter consumes hunted, but the relation is "one of reverence, of respect." You address your prey not as "it"—a score—but as "thou," an individual close to you. When you learn to do this, Campbell writes, "you can feel a change in your own psychology."

For me, each fish remains a "thou" if I catch only as many as my family would like for dinner. Sometimes they are tasty little trout from a stream that can spare them, in which case they are served with asparagus and white wine and stories—if anyone will listen. More often I release the trout and keep their stories.

Mind you, restraint comes easy for a fellow who fishes often. If your appetite is greater, may you catch all you need—as long as your prey remain creatures of flesh and blood. If they turn into scores, something has gone wrong.

Monsters

Bighorn Lake is the angler's world turned upside down, dark as outer space beneath your boat but bright at the surface and clear—so clear that a monster cruising out there is backlit by a kind of halo. If you did not know that the monster was a carp, and that carp cannot swim in air, you might wonder where lake ends and sky begins. There is no shore to keep you level, only red rock rising sheer. Springs in the canyon walls support isolated stands of aspens, but these pockets are not connected to the real world up above. If your boat were to sink, you would find no way out, no refuge but a cave. You wonder what bones might lie inside.

Curt Collins told me about the canyon last September. At the time, we were fishing the Bighorn River in its silty flatlands below the lake, where he does most of his guiding. The flow was steady, featureless, and fertile. We caught trout on deep nymphs, which is an efficient way to do it, and floated between banks lined with the world's best fly fishermen. Most of them won't try carp, Curt said—not even carp that take dry flies.

Within an hour we had left the low-church trout behind and launched into a different reality. Technically, Bighorn Lake is seventy-one miles of the Bighorn River, impounded at the mouth of the canyon. Only carp, however, have adapted to surface feeding in the profound transparent water above the dam. It is all backward.

On my first visit to that sublime geology, Curt's human company was as welcome as his angling knowledge. We crept along the border between sun and shadow, rowing where nature never intended us to go, one of us at the oars while the other cast a line in long flickering loops, aiming a dry fly at fossil monsters in the cliff and real ones in the water.

Far above us on the prairies, a herd of bison kicked up a flutter of grasshoppers which, in their rattle-brained way, flew over the precipice and down, down, down, splat. Curt and I watched one of the drowning hoppers twitching. A carp swam closer to it, and my right hand clenched the grip of my fly rod.

The rise, when it came, was nothing like that of a trout. A tubular mouth opened, moved along the surface half-submerged, and enveloped the insect in slow motion. Where the grasshopper had been there was no spreading ring—not even a dimple on the surface.

"The carp . . . is a stately, a good, and a very subtle fish," wrote Izaak Walton.

"That's a fifty-cent carp," said Curt Collins, 340 years later. Local custom, he explained, is to pass up any fish with a mouth less than nickel-sized. A tube the diameter of a quarter is worth a cast, and a silver-dollar fish on the line calls for whoops echoing off the cliffs. This is something like measuring the distance between a fish's eyes, Texas style, but Curt Collins's scale is understated. That rising carp looked to me as if it could have swallowed full-sized dill pickles. (You need conversation like this, in a place that is at once so light and so dark, to remind yourself which side you are on.)

Curt rowed me closer, softly. Motors spook the fish, he said, and the water was 520 feet too deep for a pole.

I cast at medium range, trying to avoid line splash. My hopper lit too far ahead of the fish—better than too close, because I got to try again. On my next try, the carp spotted my fly from ten feet away. Someone is going to remind me that no fish can see that far in the surface film, the window of vision being what it is, but I am reporting what happened, never mind the laws of optics. The rest was unnerving, though the carp did not zip in for the fly like a trout. ("Stately" is what Father Izaak said, if you recall. "Subtle." Not zippy.)

"*Good* fish," whispered Curt, making me twitch like a grasshopper. Curt may have feared that my soul would suffer if I hooked the very first carp I cast for. Or maybe he just enjoyed psychological warfare.

When the fish's mouth opened, I looked into a tube the diameter of a mountain bike's tires. The imitation grasshopper was slowly surrounded, engulfed, all but ingested, whereupon I struck and the hopper came back over my head with a whir. Never touched the fish.

"You tubed 'er," Curt said.

The problem, I explained, was that the carp had been swimming toward me, giving the hook no chance to find a purchase.

"The problem," Curt said, "is that you jerked it out of her mouth."

The next carp cruised in the shade of a cliff, making it harder to see, and therefore easier on my nerves.

"Lips," Curt said, and lips were exactly what we saw, rising from the black water to feed. Lips are what a carp's tube looks like from the side. My fly lit close to them and interested their owner. I lowered my rod tip, leaving slack in the line. The lips enfolded the fly and I may have twitched, but the loose line did not transmit my blunder. The lips disappeared slowly under the surface. I said "God bless America" to myself, as slowly as I could but perhaps blurring the syllables, and then struck.

"How much backing have you got?" Curt asked.

Must be a hundred yards," I guessed, because by then more than fifty were out. Between carp and me was an elegant, three-dimensional geometry that I had no time to enjoy—pale line meandering deep and dark, rod arched, fish out of touch. My tippet was seven-thousandths of an inch in diameter, which seemed flimsy, but there was no cover to tangle it. In time the back end of the fly line reappeared. From then on the carp fought at close quarters, but that first run was as powerful as anything in fresh water.

The runner was handsome in the net, too—clean and shapely in golden-olive-brown scales, a big, clean fish from big, clean water.

The word "carp" probably derives from the Greek *Kupris,* an alternative name for Aphrodite. No American would have named my fish after the goddess of love, but an English painter would have cherished it, or a Chinese. Beauty, as it turns out, is culture bound.

I opined that the tubular mouth of my conquest would fit around a big, old-fashioned silver dollar, if I had one handy. Curt conceded a Susan B. Anthony, and Curt is generous, for a fisherman. We both reckoned the fish at just more than 6 pounds.

If we had brought a scale, we could have weighed that carp with no damage. We remembered catching other carp on worms, as boys, and letting them flop around as boys used to do, and finding them wiggling on the grass an hour later, tenacious of life. We put this one back as gently as if it were a trout, but I wish now that I had taken it home and cooked it by Izaak Walton's recipe, making so curious a dish of meat as should be worth all my labor and patience.

Curt picked up his rod, next, and spotted a ring of cruising carp—daisy chain, he called it—while I practiced the art of rowing and conducting psychological operations at the same time. Look at those lips, I said. Stroke. She could eat our mustard jar without a pucker. Stroke. Good cast. She's coming! Give 'er time!

Funny thing happened then. The carp nudged the fly but did not suck it in. Curt twitched but did not strike. The fish swam away, slowly.

Within the next twenty minutes, two more carp in the chain rejected the same fly. Or maybe the same carp looked at the fly three times. Curt showed remarkable self-control, in any case, and I thought it best to stop the running commentary.

Curt reeled in his fly, picked up my rod, and cast the fly that had caught the first carp of the day. The next fish he covered took promptly—for a carp. I never did get a chance to tell Curt that he had tubed a fish.

Curt and I were both using size-8 grasshopper imitations picked from the same bin at a fly shop in Fort Smith. Mine, by pure good luck, floated low. Curt's fly was dressed a little more heavily, so he modified it—breaking up the stiff turkey wing, clipping the tail, and pulling off the legs of knotted turkey fibers. The fly then floated like a real grasshopper, and the carp were convinced. Fussy fish.

The September sun remained warm, encouraging the grasshoppers' suicide flights. The breeze was enough to carry them over the water, but not enough to make waves. Curt and I took turns at the oars and stalked another dozen monsters, of which we caught about half, which we reckoned good.

The trick was to make a presentation as cautious as that to any trout—but without getting so close that the carp saw the boat. The hull did not frighten them, but it made them curious. They would swim along at a distance, inspecting the vessel but showing no interest in our flies. Odd behavior. You don't think of fish as being inquisitive.

It turned out that Curt had designed a series of dry flies for these demanding carp. The season begins in June, he said, when cottonwood trees release their seeds to the wind. Many land on the water, where the bits of fluff float high. Midges climb onto a tuft of the cotton, thinking it a safe refuge, and fish eat protein and vegetable in one slurp. Curt has a "cotton fly" to match the hatch.

As the season wears on, carp take other insects opportunistically, like trout—with one difference, according to Curt. Trout feed on aquatic flies at all stages of their development, but carp prefer adult mayflies (spinners) when they are spent and dying on the water. Seems that the carp is not equipped to catch active prey.

I knew that, come to think of it. Here and there around the world, carp have fed on my floating flies—spent spinners in the Potomac River, for example, and moths drawn to a lighted pond in Brazil—and the rising fish have taken my imitations. In Georgetown, they used to feed on mulberries dropping from trees along the old canal. The mulberry fly was easy to tie, but using it took patience, and fly fishers are not good at patience. Not this fly fisher, anyhow.

In Bighorn Canyon, we forgot to drink the iced tea in our cooler. Who needed a stimulant? What you wanted was nerve breaks, turns at rowing while the other guy was pulling his fly away from a carp.

Made you dizzy, that gorge—ancient ocean bed, world turned on end, scaly things circling in the rifts. Casting to a shoreline is always good, even when fish are not rising, and casting to a rise is good even on open water. With ponderous fish rising next to vertical geology, the problem was sensory overload.

Have you tried to dream about trout? They are too fast, pure quicksilver, and you cannot hold them in the torpor of sleep. For dreams you need monsters, a slow drift along the cliffs at the end of the world, bright sunlight and deepest shadow.